Personal Umbrella

PERSONAL LINES COVERAGE GUIDE

Diane W. Richardson, CPCU

The National Underwriter Company

This publication is designed to provide accurate and authoritative information in regard to the subject matter covered. It is sold with the understanding that the publisher is not engaged in rendering legal, accounting, or other professional service. If legal advice or other expert assistance is required, the services of a compentent professional person should be sought. — from a Declaration of Principles jointly adopted by a Committee of the American Bar Association and a Committee of Publishers and Associations.

4157 Olympic Blvd., Suite 225
Erlanger, KY 41018

Third Printing

International Standard Book Number: 0-87218-382-3
Library of Congress Control Number: 00-132-537

Printed in The United States of America

Personal Umbrella Coverage Guide: Interpretation and Analysis

Table of Contents

Preface

The Personal Umbrella Book

As of this writing, the stock market is reaching new heights. Silicon Valley produces millionaires almost exponentially. Persons who began work a little over ten years ago at some rapid-growth companies can retire in their mid-forties; a heretofore unheard-of phenomena. New wealth is being created, and, along with that wealth comes the need to protect it.

Obviously an umbrella insurance policy is not the only wealth protection vehicle available. There are many financial products on the market. But these products will not protect the new millionaire in event of a lawsuit alleging bodily or personal injury or property damage. Unfortunately, wealthy individuals are often targets. Who would be more likely to be sued in event of a car accident, Bill Gates (yes, *that* Bill Gates) or Suzy Gates, proud driver of an '86 Chevette?

This is not to say that only the wealthy are targets. Far from it. In today's litigious society, anyone is fair game. In 1997, the most recent year for which statistics are available, there were some 15,400,000 civil suits filed in the state courts (National Center for State Courts). For the same period, there were 272,027 civil suits filed in the federal courts (Statistical Division of U.S. Courts). An umbrella can serve to protect the assets for the wealthy, and those who simply do not wish to see their assets drained because of a lawsuit.

As the need for a personal umbrella becomes greater, so does the need for the insurance professional to understand the concept and the forms. Although the Insurance Services Office (ISO) introduced a personal umbrella form in 1998, most insurers had by then already filed their own forms, and continue to use them, although at least one insurer has recently incorporated some of the ISO wording into their revised umbrella form. The American Association of Insurance Services (AAIS) has just released a personal umbrella form. Therefore, although at present there is no standardized language as there is, for example, in the common homeowners forms, this may change in the future.

Knowing what coverages are provided — indeed, even knowing where to look for the coverages (and the exclusions of coverage) in any one given form — is vital. It's too late after a claim has been presented to learn that there is no coverage, even though the term "umbrella" has led the insured to believe that coverage exists.

The purpose of this book is to acquaint the insurance professional with the common provisions, conditions, and coverages found in several personal umbrella forms. Where there are distinctive exclusions or differences in wording that lead to coverage variations, these are addressed as well. Only through understanding what is, and is not, covered, can the professional do the best job possible for the client.

Chapter 1
An Umbrella Overview

Why an Umbrella?

Auto and homeowners policies provide adequate liability protection for many people. Why, therefore, would anyone purchase an umbrella liability policy? The primary reason is to protect personal assets. Umbrellas provide an extra layer of liability coverage beyond that offered by homeowners, renters, personal auto, or stand alone personal liability policies.

Think of a young couple starting out. Both work and their combined income is good. However, being prudent, they drive older cars and save their money to purchase a home. A child enters the picture; then another. Both parents continue to work.

Because the family's income level rises, they are able to afford new vehicles and enjoy an increasingly affluent lifestyle. Since the family lives close to a large body of water, it seems reasonable to purchase a 22 foot, 150 HP inboard-out drive. The whole family enjoys a day on the water. A condo at their favorite winter vacation spot is the next purchase. It will pay for itself since they intend to rent it out during the time they don't use it themselves.

The condo is near a large winter resort area, so naturally two snowmobiles (his 'n hers) are the next purchases. They decide to allow anyone renting the condo to have access to the snowmobiles.

In the meantime, the children are growing up. The oldest, a boy, has gotten his drivers' license, and his parents have purchased a car, a four-door sedan, for him to drive to school and to his after-school job. After two years, the next child, a girl, begins to drive and her parents purchase a car for her as well.

However, she is not the safe, careful driver her brother is. She likes nothing better than to pile several of her friends in the car and cruise around.

One night someone brings a bottle along and begins passing it around. Not wishing to be thought "chicken," the daughter drinks some. She loses control of the car, and it plows into an oncoming car. A passenger in the other vehicle is killed, and two of the daughter's friends are critically injured. One recovers, but one will be paralyzed for life from the waist down.

The family's auto policy has limits for bodily injury of $100,000 per person and $300,000 per accident; and $100,000 property damage limits. The policy pays its limits, and then bows out of the picture. Homeowners liability does not apply in circumstances such as these. But the fact that the auto policy has maxed out its limits does not stop a lawsuit from the estate of the passenger in the oncoming vehicle. And friendship does not prevent a suit from the paralyzed friend's parents. After all, the family has assets (home, condo, boat, vehicles, etc.) that can be attached.

A bleak picture? Never happen?

If it seems melodramatic, consider the picture *without* the daughter's accident. What about the condo with the snowmobiles? What happens if someone runs the snowmobile into a tree, seriously injuring himself, and sues the owner for negligence? The condo owner should have known the renter didn't know how to drive a snowmobile! Or perhaps one day the son takes a few of his buddies out on the boat. As they playfully wrestle to see who can take over the wheel, the boat goes out of control and plows into a marina, totalling a Donzi 38ZX and seriously damaging a Carver 506. The family's boat owners policy has $100,000 property damage limits.

Having a personal umbrella in place might have helped alleviate some of the financial loss, as well as contribute toward defense costs.

If an imaginary scenario does not convince you of the need for an umbrella, consider this. Drivers under the age of 24 accounted for 13.6% of all licensed drivers, but for 25.5% of all accidents and 28.7% of all fatal accidents (National Safety Council, 1997). Youthful operators account for a greater proportion of accidents than the older driver, but as drivers begin to age they account for more accidents than, say, the middle-aged driver.

With the youthful operator, it is the parents' assets that must be protected; with the elderly driver, it is their own.

Sometimes an umbrella policy can involve itself in unforeseen ways. As of this writing, some six states require that uninsured/underinsured motorist coverage be offered on an umbrella policy. Arizona, Florida, Kansas, Louisianna, Nevada, and Ohio currently require that uninsured/underinsured motorist be offered on a personal umbrella. New Hampshire revised statutes 259:61 and 264:15 indicate the coverage must be offered, but in the case of *United Services Auto Association v. Wilkinson,* 569 A.2d 749 (New Hampshire 1989), the court held, with one dissention, that that had not been the intent of the legislature.

For just a few extra dollars, the policyholder can purchase an extra million (or whatever limits are selected) of uninsured/underinsured motorist coverage.

In the case of *Nationwide Mutual Insurance Co. v. Chivington et al.,* 595 N.E.2d 1002 (Ohio 1991), the appellate court held that the insured's personal umbrella policy's uninsured/underinsured motorist coverage must contribute when the insured's parents were killed in an auto accident. The facts are these: Brenton Chivington had both his own auto policy and a personal umbrella. When his parents were killed, the negligent driver's policy paid $200,000. The parents' policy, which had limits of $300,000 in uninsured/underinsured coverage, paid $100,000. The son therefore turned to his own auto policy, which provided $500,000 in uninsured/underinsured motorist coverage, and to his umbrella, which provided $1 million in uninsured/underinsured coverage. Since he had already received $300,000, his auto policy tendered $200,000; the umbrella the remaining $500,000 for a total of $1 million. (Note that uninsured/underinsured motorist coverage accrues not only for the benefit of an insured who is physically injured in an accident, but also for the benefit of someone entitled to receive damages from the person causing the bodily injury to the insured. The insured thus has a derivative claim.)

Agent Tip

In the states that require that uninsured/underinsured motorist coverage be offered on an umbrella, this case makes a strong selling point for the parents of young children to purchase an umbrella.

What is an Umbrella?

An umbrella policy provides worldwide liability coverage over and above that provided by underlying policies. For most personal lines clients, these underlying policies will be auto and homeowners. The liability coverage may be excess, or it may be "drop down." Think of a collapsed folding umbrella. When the umbrella begins to open, the shaft lengthens. That is the excess portion; the part of the umbrella that provides liability coverage over that which is already in place.

But an umbrella can provide more coverage than an excess form. As the umbrella opens, the cloth stretches over the spokes in a kind of inverted scallop pattern, protecting a much greater area than that protected by just the umbrella shaft. This broader area of coverage, that protects even where there is no underlying coverage, is often referred to as "drop down," because it drops down to protect where no underlying coverage exists. It is this "drop down" feature that distinguishes a true umbrella from an excess policy.

For example, if an insured's auto policy has limits of $250,000/$500,000 bodily injury and $250,000 property damage, when added to a $1 million umbrella the insured now has limits of $1,250,000/$1,500,000/$1,250,000. If the insured has $100,000 personal liability coverage on his or her homeowners, then, with the umbrella, there is a total of $1,100,000 in coverage. For covered occurrences not afforded coverages by the underlying policies (homeowners policies commonly do not provide personal injury coverage unless it is added by endorsement; umbrella policies include this coverage as a matter of course) the umbrella provides $1 million or whatever limit is selected, subject to the retained limit (discussed below).

What do Umbrellas Have in Common?

Lack of State Regulation

As of this writing, the only states to regulate (with the exception of requiring that uninsured/underinsured motorist coverage be offered) personal umbrellas are Texas and New York. Texas requires 10 days' notice of cancellation for non payment of premium, change in operations resulting in a hazard, or when continuation would place the insurer in violation of the Texas insurance code; otherwise 45 days' notice is required. New York regulates "personal lines insurance," such as homeowners and umbrellas, as well as auto insurance. An insurer may cancel upon giving at least 45 days' notice. Cancellation reasons include non payment of premium, conviction of a crime increasing the hazard insured against, discovery or fraud or material misrepresentation, or willful or reckless acts or omissions increasing the hazard insured against. However, the state mandates a "required policy period" of three years from the date the policy is first issued or voluntarily renewed. Nonrenewal may be only for the cancellation reasons, unless the insurer no longer does business in the state.

In nonregulated states, an insurer may cancel for any reason, although, of course, the reason must be a legitimate one, such as an increase in hazard. Depending upon the insurer, generally 10 days is given for non payment of premium; 30 days for any other reason. Notice of nonrenewal is generally 30 days.

Umbrellas are perceived as non essential insurance, unlike auto insurance, which is tied to state-mandated financial responsibility laws, or homeowners insurance, which is tied to lending institutions' requirements. Perhaps because of this, state regulators have been hesitant to become involved. Also, until recently each insurer developed its own form. In 1998 Insurance Services Office (ISO) developed a personal umbrella policy, followed in 2000 by the American Association of Insurance Services (AAIS); however, many insurers continue to use their own forms. Therefore, the coverages and exclusions found in personal umbrellas vary from insurer to insurer.

There are, however, some common elements in umbrellas. All contain *definitions*, an *insuring agreement*, *coverages* (and *exclusions*), *miscellaneous conditions*, the *duty to defend*, and the *requirement to maintain underlying insurance*. The first four common elements will be discussed in later chapters.

Duty to Defend

Often the cost of defending against a suit or claim can represent a significant expense. Umbrella policies provide defense coverage that is in addition to the limit of liability. The umbrella insurer frequently has the right to join in a defense with an underlying insurance carrier if it appears the umbrella coverage will be triggered, and sometimes will take over a defense if the underlying policy limits have been exhausted.

When a claim is outside the scope of the insurance policy's coverage, the insurer has no duty to defend. However, the duty to defend is broader than the duty to indemnify. So, if *any* allegations can be brought within the scope of the coverage, then the insurer owes the duty. As an appellate court stated, applying Missouri law, "An insurer's duty to defend exists when the petition in the underlying action states some grounds of liability covered by its insurance policy. Therefore, we must compare 'the language of the insurance contract and the allegations of the petition in the action brought by the person injured or damaged. If the complaint alleges facts which state a claim *potentially* (italics added) within the policy's coverage, there is a duty to defend.'"

The facts were these: the insured owned real estate along a river in Missouri. He sold the property to another; following the sale, the property flooded twice. The insured was sued for alleged intentional misrepresentations and negligent misrepresentation. The buyer dismissed that suit, but then filed another lawsuit alleging fraud due to intentional misrepresentations and negligent misrepresentations. This suit was dismissed with prejudice. The insured's umbrella insurer refused to defend either suit; the insured filed a damages action against his insurer.

At trial, the insurer argued that it was not required to defend for two reasons. First, the claims were not "occurrences" as defined by the policy ("'Occurrence' means an accident, including continuous or repeated exposure to substantially the same general harmful conditions, which results, during the coverage period, in 'personal injury' or 'property damage...'"). Second, the claims were excluded because of the "expected or intended" acts exclusion.

The trial court found for the insurer. But in the appeal, the court ruled for the insured, holding that the negligent misrepresentations were indeed an "occurrence" by definition, which resulted in the buyer's loss of use of the property, which was within the definition of property damage. Therefore, the insurer owed a duty to defend. The case is *Lowell K. Wood v. Safeco Insurance Company of America,* 980 S.W.2d 43 (Missouri 1998). This case will be discussed again in connection with the definition of "occurrence" in the next chapter, because in it the court considered several other jurisdictions' views.

Underlying Insurance Requirements

Umbrellas are designed to provide coverage over and above that provided by underlying policies, except, of course, when they respond to covered occurrences not addressed by the underlying insurance. The requirement to maintain underlying insurance is found within the conditions of any given umbrella form. Some insurers include as well the specific amounts of underlying insurance they require. These amounts vary. For example, one insurer may require auto liability limits of $100,000/$300,000 bodily injury and $100,000 property damage; another $100,000/$300,000/$50,000. Most insurers require at least $100,000 underlying comprehensive personal liability, although some will accept $50,000 while yet another insurer insists on $300,000. Requirements for underlying coverage for watercraft, recreational motor vehicles (other than motorcycles) and aircraft (if the underwriting guidelines allow an umbrella to be written over this exposure) vary from insurer to insurer as well.

Retained Limit

The term "retained limit" refers not only to what may be thought of as a deductible, but to the underlying limits of insurance as well. For example, a common retained limit on an umbrella is $250. So, in event of a covered auto liability loss, the insured "retains," through the underlying policy, whatever amount is required, plus the $250. Say, for example, the insured is required to maintain $300,000 single limit auto liability, and the umbrella has a $250 retained limit. A covered claim is made for $500,000. The insured "retains" $300,250 of the loss, although $300,000 of it will be covered by the underlying auto insurance. Some insurers have two retained limits, one where the claim *is* covered by underlying insurance, and another where the umbrella will provide primary coverage.

What happens if the insured fails to maintain the required underlying limit of insurance? Does the umbrella then respond on a primary basis? No. The umbrella forms usually contain language stating that the policy will still respond to a covered claim, but only to the extent it would have had the insured maintained the necessary underlying limits. This was made clear in the case of *Centennial Insurance Company v. Robert Krutek and Richard Naylor*, 1992 U.S. Dist. Lexis 19220 (Illinois 1992). In this case, Robert Krutek allegedly negligently injured Richard Naylor in an auto accident. Robert Krutek's father, with whom he resided, had an umbrella policy with limits of $2,000,000. Robert qualified as an insured under the umbrella; however, he had his own auto insurance with a bodily injury liability limit of $20,000. The umbrella required underlying auto coverage of at least $300,000 combined single limits.

The court found that the policy language was clear. The insuring agreement stated that the policy applied only in excess of the retained limit. The retained limit was defined as "the total of the applicable limits of the underlying policy(ies) listed or insurance described in Schedule A... and the applicable limits of any other underlying insurance collectible by the insured." "Retained limit" was further defined as the greater of either the above amount or $250. The court made this additional point: that the wording "applicable limit" refers to the type, rather than the collectibility, of the policy. Therefore, ruled the court, the Centennial umbrella would not apply until the amount of $320,000 in damages was reached.

Agent Tip

Before submitting an umbrella application, check carefully with the insurer regarding underwriting criteria, underlying limits requirements, etc. Because of the amount of coverage involved (the least being $1 million), often umbrella applications must be submitted unbound. It is a good practice to make sure that all policies in question — homeowners, auto, watercraft, and umbrella — have concurrent dates. It is often easiest to make the inception date for an umbrella the same as the auto; the homeowners policy period can then be adjusted to coincide with the two others. If possible, it is even more desirable to have the same insurer for all coverages. That way, there is no question as to which policy should respond first in event of a loss, and the coverages and exclusions shoud be such that there are no gaps in coverage.

The importance of watching policy dates was forcibly brought home in the case of *Commercial Union Insurance Co. v. Kevin M. Connors et al.*, 1995 Mass. Super. Lexis 603. In this case, the insureds had an umbrella policy with an expiration date of November 30, 1989. Their son was involved in an at-fault accident on December 1, 1989, and died as a result. The injured party sued his estate. Although the son's auto policy responded, the umbrella insurer informed the insureds that the policy had expired. The insureds had placed coverage through a new agency; the new agent did not send an application for a new umbrella until November 28. Remember, many insurers will not allow an agent to bind umbrella coverage. Clearly, said the court, there was no coverage.

Chapter 2

Definitions

Introduction

All umbrella forms contain definitions, the policy meaning of specified words or terms. Ideally, they should be identical to the definitions in the underlying policy(ies). But frequently they are not. And, indeed, whether or not a particular occurrence or event is covered is often first determined by checking the definitions. For example, a claimant alleges breach of fiduciary duty. A review of the definitions of "bodily injury," "personal injury," or "property damage," to which the umbrella coverage applies, indicates immediately that the umbrella is probably not the place to seek coverage.

In this chapter, we will look at how different insurers define words or terms. Several different forms form the springboard for this discussion; these are representative of the forms available. Both the Insurance Services Office (ISO) umbrella DL 98 01 06 98, and the American Association of Insurance Services (AAIS) umbrella UM 0001 01 00, forms are reprinted at the end of the book. Although, as noted, many insurers have already developed and use their own forms, these forms are useful for comparison purposes.

Bodily Injury

The first definition examined is "bodily injury." This is one of the most important definitions, because the umbrella, recall, promises to pay damages the insured is legally obligated to pay because of bodily injury or property damage arising out of a covered occurrence. Although many of the definitions are similar, be aware that not only are there differences, but additionally they are not all conveniently labeled "bodily injury." Sometimes the definition of bodily injury is included in the definition of "personal injury"; traditionally, "personal injury" has referred to nonbodily injury such as libel, although often the meaning of "personal injury" is much broader and includes not only physical injury, but any insult to the sensibilities of a person.

The first umbrella reads as follows:

"Personal injury" means:

a. bodily injury, sickness or disease, disability or shock including required care, loss of services and death resulting therefrom;

b. mental anguish or mental injury;...

Contrast this with

"Bodily injury" means bodily harm, sickness or disease, including required care, loss of services and death that results.

In the second definition, "mental anguish" is lacking. One of the most vexatious questions frequently referred to a court of law for a determination is whether or not "bodily injury" encompasses mental injury — anguish, emotional distress, outrage, and the like. Some courts have attempted to reconcile the different points of view by holding that, when mental or emotional distress results in physical manifestation of bodily injury, a claim for damages falls within the scope of coverage. For example, in the case of *Trinity Universal Insurance Company et al. v. Nicole Cowan et al.*, 945 S.W.2d 819 (Texas 1997), the court examined whether a claim for mental anguish constituted "bodily injury" and thus triggered the insurer's duty to defend. In the policy in question, "bodily injury" was defined as "bodily harm, sickness or disease. This includes required care, loss of services and death that results." The Texas supreme court concluded that, "absent an allegation of physical manifestation of mental anguish, a claim of mental anguish is not a 'bodily injury' as defined in the policy for purposes of invoking the duty to defend."

The court in *Trinity* noted that a substantial majority of those courts considering the question have held that purely mental injuries do not constitute "bodily injury," and then added an impressive body of citations to verify this. The court also added citations documenting courts that held that purely emotional injury did, in fact, constitute "bodily injury." The point is, simply, that when considering whether there is coverage for emotional distress under the definition of "bodily injury" the jurisdiction must be considered. Fortunately, as we will discuss below, the definition for "personal injury" fills much of what would otherwise be a major gap in coverage.

A definition of "bodily injury" such as that in the first definition, above, avoids such ambiguity. The definition below also avoids having an interpretation of policy language made by the courts:

"Personal injury" — means:

a. bodily injury, sickness, disease or death of any person. Bodily injury includes disability, shock, mental anguish and mental injury...

The above definition would probably avoid the problem faced by the insurer in the case of *Wolf et al. v. State Farm Insurance Co.*, 540 A.2d 871 (New Jersey 1988). The circumstances are these. Brenda Haines died from being exposed to carbon monoxide while sitting in David Phillips' car. Her father pulled her out of the car, but attempts by the life squad failed as the family watched. They filed a claim against Phillips' estate for wrongful death, survivorship, and emotional distress. The insurer stated it was only responsible for $25,000 of the $25,000/$50,000 limit, since the parents' claim was derivative of Brenda's. However, the court ruled that "such emotional distress is not the equivalent of grief from losing a loved one, but is inflicted by the trauma of seeing a loved one suffer or die or of seeing efforts to revive her being unsuccessful." In short, the emotional distress the parents suffered constituted "bodily injury" for coverage purposes.

Normally, death of a spouse leads to derivative claims for loss of consortium and services. These claims are encompassed within the applicable limit of insurance. Say, for example, that an insured is killed in an auto accident through the negligence of another. The at-fault driver has an auto policy with bodily injury limits of $100,000/$300,000. In most instances, the surviving spouse's claim for mental anguish would fall within the $100,000 limit, unlike the *Wolf* case. But wording such as that above, which includes shock and mental anguish within the definition, implies that a separate claim may be made. (Of course, umbrella limits are not split, as auto limits frequently are. Therefore, no matter how many claims are made as the result of a covered occurrence, the total limit will not be increased.)

Property Damage

The personal umbrella coverage is triggered by bodily injury, personal injury, or *property damage* caused by a covered occurrence.

> "Property damage" means physical injury to or destruction of tangible property including loss of its use.

This definition is a common one. It is like the definition for "property damage" contained in both the ISO personal auto policy and in the homeowners. For coverage to attach, tangible property must be physically injured or destroyed. Coverage also applies if the damaged property is no longer able to be used. So, for example, if an insured negligently crashes into an auto transport carrying six new Saab 9-5 wagons (MSRP $33,000) so that all the vehicles except the carrier are totaled, the umbrella will respond. If an insured negligently drives into a plate glass window of a large store so that the store is unable to open for a day while temporary repairs are being made, the policy responds to this loss of use.

Note, however, that in both the examples tangible property must be physically damaged. What happens if the property suffers no damage, yet the owner is unable to use it because of an insured's action? There is no coverage, unless the definition states, as this one does:

> "Property Damage" — means physical injury to tangible property. It includes resulting loss of use. This also means loss of use of tangible property not physically injured if the loss of use is caused by an occurrence during the policy period.

Similarly:

> Property damage means:
>
> a. physical injury or destruction of tangible property; or
>
> b. the loss of use of tangible property whether or not it is physically damaged.

With this language, there need be no physical loss to the property for there to be coverage, so long as loss of use is caused by a covered occurrence. For example, the insured, while attempting to install a lawn sprinkler system, negligently cuts an underground phone line. Worse, he also cuts into a gas pipeline. The surrounding neighborhood, including a marina, must be evacuated while the gas leak is brought under control and the pressure checked. There is no damage to the neighborhood property or the marina; but there is loss of use of the tangible property. Since the insured's negligence in this case is a covered occurrence (the definition of "occurrence" is discussed below), the resulting loss of use is covered up to the applicable limits.

Personal Injury

The next definition to be considered is that for "personal injury." "Personal injury" in insurance has traditionally referred to nonbodily injury; that is, injury to the mental well-being of the person. Use of the term to describe bodily injury has become more and more common, however. One need only look at the attorneys' ads in the yellow pages. ("Personal Injury! Workers' Compensation!" is the top line, followed by: "Auto/ Motorcycle Accidents, Dog Bites/Slip and Fall, Wrongful Death, Work Related Injuries...")

Agent Tip

Check carefully to see that the umbrella clearly defines what the insurer means by "personal injury." Since many homeowners forms do not automatically include this coverage, it is one of the more important "drop down" coverages, and a powerful reason to purchase an umbrella.

The first form defines "personal injury" thus:

"Personal injury" means:

a. injury arising out of one or more of the following offenses:

(1) false arrest, detention or imprisonment, or malicious prosecution or humiliation;

(2) libel, slander or defamation of character; or

(3) invasion of privacy, wrongful eviction or wrongful entry.

Contrast the above definition with the following. Consider which definition is broadest.

Nonbodily injury means false arrest, invasion of privacy, wrongful eviction or entry, libel, slander, or defamation of character.

Lacking here is "[false] detention or imprisonment, or malicious prosecution or humiliation." Perhaps not an important distinction, until the insured is faced with a claim that normally would be covered by "personal injury," such as malicious prosecution.

The next definition to discuss is:

"Personal injury" means injury arising out of one or more of the following offenses:

1. False arrest, detention or imprisonment;

2. Malicious prosecution;

3. The wrongful eviction from, wrongful entry into, or invasion of the right of private occupancy of a room, dwelling or premises that a person occupies, committed by or on behalf of its owner, landlord or lessor.

4. Oral or written publication of material that slanders or libels a person or organization or disparages a person's or organization's goods, products or services; or

5. Oral or written publication of material that violates a person's right of privacy.

This definition contains the same elements as the first; however, lacking is the inclusion of "humiliation" and "defamation of character" which appears to leave a gap. But if we consider that defamation of character usually arises from libel or slander, this should not present a problem. There is another possible gap, however. Invasion of privacy can take more forms than invasion of the right of private occupancy of a place, so this part of the definition is something to take note of.

The following definition is broader still:

"Personal injury" — means:

a. false arrest; false imprisonment; wrongful detention; wrongful entry; invasion of rights of occupancy; or malicious prosecution;

b. libel; slander; misrepresentation; humiliation; defamation of character; invasion of rights of privacy; and

c. discrimination and violation of civil rights, where recovery is permitted by law. Fines and penalties imposed by law are not included.

This definition is extremely broad in that the inclusion of "discrimination and violation of civil rights" could encompass a variety of offenses (but not those arising out of business activities. See Chapter 6 for a discussion of this exclusion). It should be noted that the above definition is found in a policy which does not include "farming" within the definition of "business", thus affording broader coverage than most umbrellas. Farming aside, say an insured owns a duplex and rents the unit she does not reside in. However, since she herself is elderly, she does not wish to rent to a family with more than one or two small children. If she is sued because of this, presumably (the "presumably" will be discussed below) the definition will trigger the policy's response.

One of the potential gaps in the definition discussed prior to the above is closed here, and that is the inclusion of *both* "invasion of rights of occupancy" and "invasion of rights of privacy."

"Personal Injury" and the Courts

Determining the scope of "personal injury" coverage has proven almost as vexacious for the courts as deciding whether bodily injury and mental injury are linked. The problem, as evidenced in the cases discussed below, is how much the coverage is bounded by the exclusion (discussed in Chapter 6) for intentionally harmful acts. For example, since "malice" is defined in *Webster's Collegiate Dictionary (Tenth Edition)* as "desire to cause pain, injury, or distress to another," how can one commit *unintentional* "malicious prosecution"?

In the case of *Hain et al. v. Allstate Insurance Co.*, 471 S.E.2d 521 (Georgia 1996), the appellate court found the jury had not erred in granting summary judgment to the insurer. The insured had a homeowners and an umbrella policy with Allstate. He was sued for assault and battery and intentional infliction of emotional distress stemming from a pattern of sexual harassment that, said the claimant, occurred both in and away from the workplace. The complaint alleged that the insured acted "with the specific intent to cause [the claimant] harm." The court held that the umbrella specifically excluded coverage for acts intended to cause bodily injury, including mental anguish. Further, stated the court, "assault and battery and intentional infliction of emotional distress are by their very nature intentional torts." Therefore, the judgment for the insurer was affirmed.

But in the case of *Frank V. Purrelli v. State Farm Fire and Casualty Company*, 698 So. 2d 618 (Florida 1997), the appellate court viewed the coverage and the exclusion, found the policy ambiguous, and found for the insured. The insured was sued for invasion of privacy. He allegedly took inappropriate videos of a female employee, who was also a patient, during chiropractic treatment sessions. (Policies do not commonly exclude boorish behavior.) The trial court ruled in favor of the insurer, ruling that the personal umbrella did not provide coverage for an invasion of privacy. But the appellate court determined the policy was ambiguous, since "[it] defined personal injury to explicitly include 'invasion of rights of privacy' and eleven other intentional torts, including assault and battery, false arrest, false imprisonment, libel, slander, and defamation of character. The policy contained a provision excluding personal injuries that were 'expected or intended'... The policy purports to insure invasion of privacy, an intentional tort, but excludes acts 'intended' by the insured and limits coverage to 'accidents'.'' (A common problem with the personal umbrella. For the way in which one insurer circumvents this, see Chapter 6.) Further, said the court, "an insurance contract that explicitly covers the intentional tort of invasion of privacy but limits coverage to 'accidents' is ambiguous." So stating, the court reversed the trial court and remanded for further proceedings.

The court in *Purrelli*, above, looked to the case of *Byron C. Bailer et al. v. Erie Insurance Exchange*, 687 A.2d 1375 (Maryland 1995), for guidance in rendering its decision. The insured had a personal umbrella policy. He and his wife hired an *au pair*. One day, the husband surreptitiously video-taped the woman showering. When she learned of the action, the woman left her employment and filed suit against both husband and wife for invasion of privacy. The Bailers sought defense and indemnification by Erie, but Erie declined. The Bailers then engaged their own attorney to settle the claim with the *au pair*, and brought action against Erie. The trial court granted Erie's motion for summary judgment, and this action resulted.

The policy defined "personal injury" as including "invasion of privacy, or humiliation caused by any of these." The insureds argued that, at the very least, the policy was ambiguous because it expressly insured against invasion of privacy. The insurer argued that there was no ambiguity because the policy should be construed to cover negligent invasion of privacy and exclude intentional invasion. Illogically, the insurer then argued that even if invasion of privacy was exclusively an intentional tort (which most jurisdictions hold) and even if the policy covered intended conduct that produced unintended results, the injury in this case was intended so the exclusion should apply.

In a well-reasoned response, finding for the insured, the Maryland appellate court looked both to the underlying homeowners policy and to the umbrella. Stated the court, "the types of tort liabilities such as malicious prosecution, slander, and invasion of privacy which are specifically included within the insuring provision of the catastrophe policy ordinarily are not covered under insuring provisions of the type found in Erie's basic homeowners's policy. This is because these torts typically do not involve bodily injury... or because these torts do not involve an accident... The insuring provision in the Bailers' catastrophe policy differs from that in their underlying homeowner's policy.... The catastrophe policy enlarges the coverage from 'bodily injury' to 'personal injury' and then defines the latter term specifically to include certain enumerated torts among which is invasion of privacy." The ambiguity thus led to coverage.

Occurrence

The insuring agreements of many personal umbrella policies promise to pay damages the insured is legally obligated to pay for bodily injury, personal injury, or property damages arising out of an occurrence. What, therefore, is an "occurrence"?

> "Occurrence" means an accident, including continuous or repeated exposure to substantially the same general harmful conditions, which results, during the policy period, in:
>
> (1) "bodily injury"; or
>
> (2) "property damage".

This definition is a familiar one; indeed, it appears in the ISO homeowners form. But, as noted above, an ambiguity arises when "occurrence" defined as an "accident" does not address personal injury. The form quoted above, in the insuring agreement, promises to pay damages for "'personal injury' for which an 'insured' becomes legally liable due to one or more offenses listed under the definition of 'personal injury' to which this insurance applies." With this language, the ambiguity is circumvented. However, this is not the case in all the forms examined.

In the case of *Lowell K. Wood v. Safeco Insurance Company of America*, 980 S.W.2d 43 (Missouri 1998), the question revolved around whether negligent misrepresentation was an accident, and therefore within the scope of an "occurrence" for coverage purposes (the details of the case were given in Chapter 1). The Missouri appellate court looked to Maryland in finding for the insured, quoting with approval the finding in *Sheets v. Brethren Mutual Ins. Co.*, 679 A.2d 540 (Maryland 1996): "If we were to adopt an objective standard and hold that the term 'accident' as used in liability insurance policies excludes coverage for damage that should have been foreseen or expected by the insured, such insurance policies would be rendered all but meaningless. Under such an interpretation, the policy would provide no coverage for negligent acts resulting in objectively foreseeable or expectable damage. Only acts of negligence resulting in objectively unforeseeable or unexpectable damage would be covered. Of course, under basic principles of tort law, the insured is unlikely to be held liable for unforeseeable or unexpectable damages resulting from his negligence. Thus, interpreting 'accident' as encompassing only negligent acts resulting in unforeseeable and unexpected damages would leave the insured covered against only those damages for which he or she is not likely to be held liable. We decline to adopt such a restrictive construction of the term accident."

The court in *Wood* also looked at the case of *Safeco Ins. Co. of America v. Andrews*, 915 F.2d 500 (California 1990), which also involved a case of negligent misrepresentation, but found that the finding for the insurer was not convincing since the court did not explain its reasoning; stating merely that "the cause of damage was [the insured's] alleged misrepresentations, which are not an 'occurrence' or a 'peril insured against' under the policy."

Agent Tip

Check the umbrella language carefully to make sure any possible ambiguity between coverages and exclusions is resolved. It is unwise to rely on an insurer stating what it really *intends* to cover; form language controls in event of a suit going to court, not intentions.

"Occurrence" means:

a. an accident, including continuous or repeated exposure to substantially the same general harmful conditions, which results, during the coverage period, in:

   (1) personal injury; or

   (2) property damage;

b. an offense, committed during the coverage period, which results in personal injury.

This definition also avoids ambiguity by including "an offense committed during the coverage period, which results in personal injury" within the definition of an occurrence. Of course, note that the offense must be committed within the coverage period; obviously the policy will not respond to an insured libeling someone and then purchasing an umbrella to cover the ensuing action.

Business

For the most, the personal umbrella is not intended to cover activities associated with an insured's business. (Business-related exclusions and exceptions will be examined in Chapter 6.) Look at the following two definitions:

"Business" means a trade, profession or occupation.

> "Business" includes trade, profession, or occupation.

These are common definitions. Unfortunately, they can lead to confusion on the part of the insured. If "business *means* [italics added] a trade, profession, or occupation," does "business" mean part-time activities for money that are not the insured's trade, profession, or occupation? On the other hand, if "business *includes* [italics added] trade, profession, or occupation, then are part-time activities excluded? One insurer solves the dilemma with this language:

> "Business" — means any full or part-time activity of any kind engaged in for economic gain. It does not include:
>
> a. farming; or
>
> b. the rental or holding for rental of any premises in a one, two, three or four family residence owned or controlled by an insured as a dwelling, office, school, or studio.

Note that, in this case, both full and part-time occupations fall into the defintion of a business, except for farming. Note as well that incidental rental of premises the insured owns (or controls) for office, studio or school purposes falls outside this definition. This exception — whereby rental or holding for rental of an insured location for use in part as an office, school or studio is not considered a business — is similar to that found in the homeowners section II liability business exclusion.

The courts generally hold that, to constitute a "business," two elements must be present: a continuity or recurrent character of the activity, and a profit motive. Therefore, it appears that activities incidental to a business — those that are usual to nonbusiness activities — are covered. However, it is all too often left to the courts to determine whether particular activities fall within or outside the definition.

Some umbrella forms make the definition of "business" narrower so that the form can be used to cover farming activities; depending, of course, on underwriting acceptance. The definition above is one such; another reads:

> Business includes but is not limited to a trade, occupation, profession or other activity engaged in as a means of livelihood or from which you or a relative intend to derive income (other than farming).

Although, in this definition, farming is exempted and is therefore covered, the problem is with the wording "you or a relative intend to derive income." At what point can, say, a hobby fall into this definition with the result that coverage is excluded? Say, for example, an insured is an exceptionally clever landscape gardener. She toys with the idea of starting a business, and goes so far as to submit a business plan to the Small Business Administration. Before anything further is accomplished, she begins to landscape, as a birthday gift, a friend's home. In the course of the work, she accidentally severs an underground power line, with the result that several homes in the neighborhood are without power. Is the fact that she hopes, sometime in the future, to derive income enough to preclude coverage? Or must the "intent" have more concrete support? Unfortunately, this question is not resolved in the form itself, nor has it been resolved in the courts as of this writing.

Motor Vehicles

The final definition to consider is "motor vehicle." At this point, we will only examine the different definitions; in Chapter 4 we will look at who is insured for use of a motor vehicle, what is excluded, etc. There is one common element: in the forms examined, motorized vehicles designed to assist the handicapped and motorized vehicles used to service a residence premises are not addressed. Since the underlying homeowners forms give coverage to such vehicles, there is no need.

As noted earlier, there is no standard personal umbrella form. It follows, therefore, that definitions will not be standardized. In one form, definition is almost by default; that is, the definition shows up in the required underlying insurance condition:

> Automobile — ownership, maintenance or use of any land motor vehicle. This includes any machinery or equipment attached to the vehicle. It does not include a recreational motor vehicle.
>
> Recreational Motor Vehicle — ownership, maintenance or use of a land motor vehicle:
>
> a. not subject to motor vehicle registration; and
>
> b. designed for recreational use off public roads.

In this definition, an auto includes a van, pickup, private passenger vehicle, motorcycle, or a farm tractor and an attached farm implement. A recreational motor vehicle includes a golf cart, snowmobile or all-terrain vehicle. This definition is used in the same form that excepts farming from a business, so it is logical that a farm tractor will be given coverage.

Some forms avoid any misinterpretation through simplicity:

> Automobile means a motorized land vehicle and includes trailers, semi-trailers, farm tractors, trailers and implements.

Under this definition, any motorized land vehicle — recreational, subject to motor vehicle registration or not — is included.

The following form refines the definition into automobile, private automobile, and recreational motor vehicle:

> "Automobile" means a land motor vehicle, trailer or semi-trailer designed for use mainly on public roads. This does not include recreational motor vehicles, farm tractors, trailers or implements.

> "Private automobile" means an automobile other than a truck-tractor, its trailer or semi-trailer, or a truck with load capacity of 1-1/2 or more tons. A truck, pick-up, panel or van body vehicle or its trailer is not a private automobile while being used for wholesale or retail pick-ups or deliveries.

> "Recreational motor vehicle" means a recreational land motor vehicle designed for use off public roads. This includes a motorized all terrain vehicle, amphibious vehicle, dune buggy, golfmobile, snowmobile, trailbike, or minibike.

Note that tractors fall outside the definition of an automobile. Because of the definition, and because there is no further exclusion, use of tractors is covered. Note as well that "automobile" is a broad, all-encompassing term which is narrowed into "private automobile." Of the umbrella forms examined, this is the only one that gives a size limit for a truck to fit the definition of a "private auto."

Agent Tip

A cautionary word of advice! Definitions do not coverage make. For example, the above definition for "automobile" might lead the insured to think that there is coverage for driving a tractor trailer. This is not necessarily the case. In this particular form, any loss arising out of the insured's business operations involving an "automobile" is excluded. Therefore, when reviewing definitions, keep in mind that the coverage will be bounded by any pertinent limitations and exclusions.

The final definition considered below separates the definitions into two parts:

> "Auto" means:

1. A private passenger motor vehicle, motorcycle, moped or motor home; or

2. While towed by a private passenger motor vehicle, a trailer, farm wagon or farm implement.

"Recreational motor vehicle" means:

1. All-terrain vehicle;

2. Dune buggy;

3. Golf cart;

4. Snowmobile; or

5. Any other motorized land vehicle which is designed for recreational use off public roads.

Tractors are not included in this definition; if a tractor is viewed as a vehicle not licensed for road use and used to service the premises, then coverage attaches through the homeowners. Possibly the form is not intended for the farm owner. And, although the definition for "auto" includes a moped or motorcycle, and thus appears to provide broad coverage, there are endorsements that an underwriter may use to exclude specific autos, recreational vehicles, or watercraft under this particular umbrella form.

Obviously, not all definitions in all the common forms have been discussed. Particularly notable by its absence is "insured," which we look at next in Chapter 3.

Chapter 3

Who Is An Insured?

Introduction

As noted earlier, the chief reason to purchase a personal umbrella policy is to protect one's assets. Personal umbrella policies promise to pay damages for which an insured becomes legally liable in event of a covered occurrence. Therefore, knowing who will be covered in event of a loss is vital. The following chapter will look at the wording used in different forms to describe an insured person, except for who is an insured for use of a motor vehicle or watercraft. This will be discussed in Chapters 4 and 5.

Agent Tip

The prudent agent will regularly update information on umbrella insureds regarding who resides in the insured's home. Are there stepchildren? Is there shared custody? Do the insureds provide foster care?

The Named Insured and Spouse

In determining who is covered under any given umbrella, it is often necessary to look in different places in the policy. It is common to preface the definitions with wording such as this:

> Throughout the policy, "you" and "your" refer to the "named insured" shown in the Declarations and the spouse if a resident of the same household....

Likewise:

> In this endorsement the words "you," "your" or "yours" mean the person named in the declarations and his or her spouse who lives in the same household.

Similarly:

> Throughout this policy, the words "you," "your," and "yours," mean each person named on the Coverages Page, and his or her spouse if they live together.

Clarifying that coverage applies to the named insured and spouse if they reside in the same household avoids questions of coverage should the marriage terminate and one of the parties vacate the marital home. Without this provision, the insurer could conceivably provide liability coverage to two households for one premium.

According to *Black's Law Dictionary, Fifth Edition*, a "spouse" is "one's wife or husband." Currently, umbrella forms do not address other relationships between adults. Two unmarried adults who are desireous of umbrella coverage and who share living arrangements would each have to be shown as named insureds, if the insurer's underwriting practices permit.

The ISO personal auto policy (PAP), 1998 edition, extends coverage in the event a spouse ceases to be a resident of the household for a period of the earlier of: (a) the end of 90 days following the spouse's change of residency; (b) the effective date of another policy listing the spouse as a named insured; or (c) the end of the policy period. Therefore, the spouse continues to be a named insured during this time, and thus covered on the auto policy. However, there is currently no such provision in the homeowners forms, nor in any of the umbrella forms reviewed.

Agent Tip

It might be prudent, in event this situation occurs, to check with the underwriter to see if coverage can be extended until a separate umbrella policy is in place.

An interesting case involving both a homeowners and an umbrella policy found the homeowners insurer attempting to prove a divorced wife *was* an insured, and the insured and the umbrella insurer attempting to prove she was *not*, under the homeowners policy. The facts are these. Husband and wife divorced, and the wife moved out of the marital home, relinquishing all right, title and interest in the property. Her name, however, was not deleted from the homeowners policy as a named insured. About four months later, the couple got into a fight on the insured premises, and the ex-wife was injured. She sued her ex-husband for bodily injury in state court. The homeowners insurer, Independent Fire, declined to defend the ex-husband, citing the policy exclusion for bodily injury to insureds. The umbrella insurer, United Fire, agreed to provide a defense but under a reservations of rights. It then brought a declaratory judgment action to determine the rights and obligations of the parties under the two policies.

Even though the ex-wife had moved out, the Louisiana appellate court in *United Fire & Casualty v. Reeder et al.*, 9 F.3d 15 (1993), found for the homeowners insurer, Independent Fire, and held that the ex-wife was still a named insured. The court recognized that she had relinquished interest in the property. However, stated the court, "[The wife] was exposed to the risk of liability at the time of her injury. She had moved out of the ... house only a few months earlier. A third party incurring injury on the premises might have blamed a condition that [she] created before she left. [She] possessed the requisite interest — potential legal liability." Therefore, the homeowners exclusion held.

Agent Tip

Be very careful if the insureds, as is sometimes now the case, have deeded the family residence to a living trust. Although there are ways to address the homeowners exposure, there are, as of this writing, few insurers who offer a way to modify a personal umbrella to cover a non-living entity.

Family Members — Who are They?

Having determined that the named insured and spouse are the "you" referred to before the definitions, the next place to see who is covered is in the definitions themselves. Even here, some insurers define "insured" as "you" (discussed above) and "members of your household" or "members of your family," or simply "relatives," which necessitates finding another definition. For example:

"Insured" means you and also:

a. any member of your household.

"Member of your household" means any person whose principal place of residence is the same as yours and who is:

a. related to you by blood, marriage or adoption; or

b. a ward or foster child.

Similarly:

"Insured" means:

1. You.

2. A "family member."

"Family member" means a resident of your household who is:

1. Your relative, including a ward or foster child; or

2. Under the age of 21 and in the care of you or an "insured" who is age 21 or over.

These definitions are similar to those found in both homeowners and auto policies, although, note that in the definition above, "relative" is not defined. But since a "relative" is usually defined as a person related by marriage, blood, or adoption, simply referring to "your relative" should not prove a problem. A person who is not a relative, ward or foster child can qualify as an insured, but only if they are both under 21 and in the care of the named insured or another family member who is over 21.

One umbrella form circumvents possible discrepancies between underlying policy definitions by stating that:

> Except as stated within this definition, insured means all persons or entities covered by underlying insurance. Each such person or entity is a separate insured, but this does not increase our limit.

According to *Black's Law Dictionary, Fifth Edition*, "The meaning of [the] word 'family' necessarily depends on [the] field of law in which word is used, purpose intended to be accomplished by its use, and facts and circumstances of each case... Most commonly refers to group of persons consisting of parents and children; father, mother and their children; immediate kindred, constituting fundamental social unit in civilized society." Whether for coverage or exclusionary purposes, however, questions of relationship rarely arise. The question that *does* arise, though, is what constitutes a "residence." Further, what constitutes a *principal* place of residence? This issue has often been addressed by the courts with varying outcomes.

What is a Residence?

There are two common situations where the question of residency arises. The first of these is where a child attends a school or college and lives away from the parental home for much of the year. The second situation involves children of divorced parents.

Student Away at School

The Insurance Services Office (ISO) homeowners 2000 form contains a more restrictive definition of "insured" than those above:

> "Insured" means:
>
> a. You and residents of your household who are:
>
> (1) Your relatives; or
>
> (2) Other persons under the age of 21 and in the care of any person named above.
>
> b. A student enrolled in school full time, as defined by the school, who was a resident of your household before moving out to attend school, provided the student is under the age of:
>
> (1) 24 and your relative; or
>
> (2) 21 and in your care or the care of a person described in a.(1) above...

Graduate students in a doctoral program, or 22-year old wards who are attending school full time, conceivably are without coverage under this definition, even though all other critera — parental financial support, what the student considers his or her permanent address, etc. — are present. If this definition is in the underlying homeowners policy, then other coverage should be arranged lest there be a gap. Although current umbrella forms are not this restrictive, a court is often an expensive place to prove a point. And, as demonstrated in the cases below, the courts are mixed.

In the case of *The Midwestern Indemnity Company v. Gerald Craig, et al.*, 665 N.E.2d 712 (Ohio 1995), uninsured/underinsured motorist coverage under an umbrella would not be triggered if the student away at school was not an insured. The facts are these. Jeffrey Gordon lived with his mother and stepfather, Carol and Gerald Craig. He was seriously injured in an auto accident; the at-fault driver's policy paid its limit of $100,000. However, Jeffrey's injuries exceeded that amount, so he sought additional coverage under both his own auto policy and his stepfather's umbrella policy.

The insurer denied coverage, holding that Jeffrey was not an insured. But the trial court, and later the Ohio court of appeals affirmed, that Jeffrey was an insured despite his status as a student away at school. The trial court, citing *Black's Law Dictionary*, explained its reasoning: "The term family was 'not confined to those who stand in a legal or blood relationship, but rather should include those who live within the domestic circle of, and are economically dependent on, the named insured...'" To support its determination, the court found that Mrs. Craig provided financial support — tuition, books, rent, utilities, food and clothing, medical care, and car insurance. Further, Jeffrey had a room in the home and returned there on several weekends and during college recesses.

But in the case of *Quincy Mutual Fire Insurance Company v. Stephen Clyman, et al.*, 910 F. Supp. 230 (Pennsylvania 1996), the district court viewed much the same evidence, and yet held that student Kenneth was not an insured under his parents' homeowners policy. Kenneth allegedly tripped over a dog toy that had been left on the stairs of his parents' home, and was injured. He sued his parents, alleging their negligence caused his injury. The insurer declined coverage, citing the exclusion for "bodily injury to you or an insured," and holding that Kenneth was an insured by definition ("residents of your household who are your relatives").

The record showed that Kenneth was a full-time student away at school in Arizona, received financial support for tuition and books, an allowance, and health insurance, and was listed as a dependent on his parents' tax returns. Kenneth himself, although he held an Arizona driver's license and registered his car in Arizona, listed his parents' address on all school-related papers and did not apply for Arizona resident status, which would have entitled him to a reduced tuition. He spent college breaks at the family home. Yet, the court held that this evidence was inconclusive. The court held that, in Pennsylvania, a relative must actually have regular, personal contact in order to be considered a resident. And, since Kenneth spent some ten months of the year elsewhere, he was not a resident of the named insured's household.

Children of Divorce

One of the cases *Quincy Mutual*, above, looked to was the case of *Amica Mutual Insurance Company v. Donegal Mutual Insurance Company*, 545 A.2d 343 (Pennsylvania 1988). Here, the court distinguished between "domicile" and "residence"; "domicile being that place where a man has his true, fixed and permanent home and principal establishment, and to which whenever he is absent he has the intention of returning. Residence being a factual place of abode. Living in a particular place, requiring only physical presence."

Elizabeth Hagerty, 18, was operating a car with two passengers in it when an accident occurred, injuring all three. One of the passengers sued. A declaratory judgment action between Amica Mutual, Elizabeth's mother's insurer, and Donegal Mutual, her father's insurer, followed. Elizabeth had resided with her father during 1982, but resided with her mother for the school year 1983-1984, even though she continued to keep clothes and personal belongings at her father's, and received mail there as well. Further, Elizabeth intended to return to her father's residence.

The court stated that although "domicile" and "residence" could be used in the same context, without "additional words of refinement, i.e., permanent, legal, etc.," "resident" carried a more transitory meaning. Therefore, residence became a matter of physical fact. It was a matter of physical fact that Elizabeth resided with her mother at the time of the accident; the mother's policy applied, not the father's. Thus, the concept of "residence" (which was in keeping with the policy language) took precedence over the concept of "domicile."

The court in *Peggy Mobley v. State Farm Mutual Automobile Ins. Co.*, 674 So.2d 1117 (Louisiana 1996), construed this policy language: "Relative — means a person related to you or your spouse by blood, marriage or adoption who lives with you" and noted that it differed from many prior policies it had seen; that is, the policy did not define a relative as "resident of the same household." The Louisiana court of appeals did not find the language ambiguous, and so the insurance contract should be enforced as written.

In this case, the insured's daughter Courtney was injured when a car she alighted from rolled over her foot. The driver was underinsured, so Courtney's mother, with whom she lived at the time of the accident, sought coverage under both her own State Farm auto policy and her estranged husband's State Farm auto and umbrella policies. In finding for the insurer that Courtney did *not* live with her father, and so there was no coverage under her father's policy, the court stated: "We find that some of the factors that determine whether a child lives with the named insured include, but are not limited to (1) where the child spends his time when not employed or at school; (2) where the child keeps his or her clothing or other personal belongings; (3) where the child receives his or her mail, including official notices and mail from friends; and (4) whether the child has a bedroom in the parent's house. Of course, these factors are not exclusive, nor is any one factor more determinative than another. Consideration should also be given to the fact that a child may 'live with' each separated or divorced parent under a joint custody plan."

Quoting the above language with approval, particularly the last sentence, in reaching quite a different decision for the plaintiff was the Louisiana appellate court in the case of *Robert J. Carbon v. Allstate Insurance Company*, 701 So. 2d 462 (Louisiana 1997). In this case, Jennifer Carbon was seriously injured when she was thrown from a vehicle driven by a drunken driver. Jennifer's parents were divorced at the time of the accident, but they were awarded joint care, custody, and control. However, at the time of the accident, she was living with her mother in Texas.

Jennifer's father Robert Carbon sought underinsured motorist coverage under both his auto and umbrella policies, which provided coverage for relatives of the named insured who resided in the named insured's household. The policies defined "resident" as "the physical presence in your household with the intention to continue living there. Unmarried dependent children, while temporarily away from home will be considered residents if they intend to continue to live in your household." The trial court ruled the language ambiguous and against public policy and found for Robert Carbon; Allstate appealed.

The court noted that the intent of a child's parents regarding residence, and not the intent of the child herself, was determinative. The parents, being "natural tutors," had the right to designate a child's residence. However, in the case of joint custody, the parents gave the right to establish residence to the court, and therefore the child's residence was with both parents as a matter of law. Distinguishing from *Hagerty*, above, the court said that whether a person was or was not a resident of a household was a question of law as well as of fact (*Hargety* viewed only the fact of the daughter's physical presence in the household at the time of the accident). Stating that the judgment awarding joint custody also demonstrated that Jennifer was to reside with each parent, the court upheld the trial court's finding that Jennifer was a resident of her father's household, and therefore entitled to coverage.

Status of a Ward or Foster Child

The wording of personal umbrella policies, as well as underlying homeowners and auto policies, makes it clear that, for coverage purposes, wards and foster children are accorded "insured" status. Therefore, if a ward or foster child in the named insured's custody were to negligently injure someone — say, cause another child at school to trip and fall down a flight of stairs — there would be coverage. But the "down side" to this is that because of the ward's or foster child's status as an insured, should the ward or foster child become injured because of the named insured's negligence, and a suit brought claiming damages for the child, there is no coverage for the named insured because of the intra-family exclusion.

Agent Tip

If any insureds care for foster children, they should make sure the agency placing the children has coverage in place that would protect the insureds should such a situation arise.

Adult "Children"

The U.S. district court in *Allstate Insurance Company v. Mary Jane Sprout et al.*, 782 F. Supp. 999 (Pennsylvania 1991) looked at *Amica*, above, in distinguishing "domicile, that is, the place where one has voluntarily fixed his habitation along with an intention to stay there for the indefinite future" from "residence, a separate and distinct concept which does not take into account the intention of the person involved." A car driven by Frank Potter crossed the center line into oncoming traffic, and Nicole Sprout, a passenger in the car, was killed. At the time of the accident Potter's parents, the Bairs, had a personal auto policy and an umbrella with Allstate. The defendants attempted to prove that, at the time of the accident, Potter was a resident of his parents' household and therefore the policies should afford coverage.

In looking at *Amica*, the court said the appropriate concept in this instance was "residence," since the policy stated that an unmarried dependent child would be considered a resident relative while temporarily away from home if they intended to resume residing in the named insured's household. The defendants argued that Potter had moved out of his parents' home twice before, and was welcome back at any time. But the court noted that there was no evidence that Potter's moving out of his parents' home was temporary. He was employed and lived first with his sister and then at a motel, although, at the time of the accident all rooms there had been rented and so he checked out. However, there was contradictory evidence that he had returned to his parents' home. Therefore, said the court in holding for *Allstate*, the term "resident" was clear; a person "must actually live in the household and must not just be passing through."

But "passing through" was exactly the case in *State Farm Fire & Casualty Co. v. The Estate of Kenneth John Lazio et al.*, 822 F. Supp. 660 (California 1993), yet the court held that Kenneth Lazio was a resident of his parents' household. Lazio's parents had a personal umbrella policy with State Farm which covered "the following residents of the named insured's household: (1) the named insured's relatives..." At the time of his death, Kenneth Lazio was 29. He had moved out of his parents' home in 1981, and in 1987 had purchased a home with his brother. The home was sold a few weeks prior to his death. Lazio was planning either to buy a new home, build one in Arizona, or possibly move in with a girlfriend. After selling his home, he asked his parents if he could live with them for a time, to which the parents agreed.

But following the home's sale, Lazio moved his possessions into a storage unit and left for a vacation in Arizona. He returned, and for one night slept in a sleeping bag on his parents' living room floor. He died the next night in a motorcycle accident, along with a passenger. Suit was brought on behalf of the passenger's daughter, seeking damages for wrongful death. The insurer sought a judgment declaring that it had no duty to defend or indemnify the estate.

The court looked at the cases State Farm presented where the court had considered the effect of the household resident language in insurance policies, but held they were all distinguishable from the case at bar. The California district court held that Lazio's residency in the named insured's house was on an indefinite, although temporary, basis at the time the accident occurred. The evidence was clear that Lazio had no address or residence other than that of his parents. Applying California law, the court noted with approval the case of *Hardware Mutual Casualty Company v. Home Indemnity Company,* 241 Cal. App. 2d 303 (1966), which held that "a resident of the same household is one, other than a temporary or transient visitor, who lives together with others in the same house for a period of some duration, although he may not intend to remain there permanently." So saying, the court found coverage.

Married, with (Married) Children

The next situation to be discussed is what happens, as is often the case, when married children (and their families) return to the parental home following, say, a corporate down-sizing. As was the case with unmarried children such as those discussed above, when the facts would seem to warrant agreement, the courts in the cases discussed below reach completely different conclusions.

The Tischhausers' daughter and her husband and children (the Clevelands) arrived at the Tischhausers' mobile home to stay until the husband could find work. During the time the Clevelands had been married, they stayed temporarily with the Tischhausers a number of times when they were having financial difficulties.

On this occasion, they arrived at the Tischhausers' mobile home with their belongings in a trailer. They unloaded their belongings and placed them in a garage on the premises, where they remained, except for some clothing, for the next several weeks. After unpacking the trailer, James Cleveland and the Tischhausers left to return the trailer. During the time they were gone, Douglas, one of the Cleveland children, started a fire that destroyed the mobile home and its contents, as well as property of a neighbor. The neighbors sued. The trial court found, and the Oregon court of appeals affirmed, that the Clevelands were temporary guests of the Tischhausers, and not members of their household. Said the court in *Guenther H. Lang et al. v. Foremost Insurance Company*, 778 P.2d 510 (Oregon 1989), "The evidence permits the conclusion that, although the Clevelands' stay was to be of an indefinite length, it was not to be permanent and that the Clevelands were only financially dependent (the Tischhausers paid the Clevelands' living expenses) until James found employment. The evidence also supports a finding that the Clevelands and the Tischhausers were separate family units."

The evidence in the case above would appear to provide more of a basis for coverage than did that presented in *Lazio*, yet the court reached a different conclusion.

Finally, a look at a case that reached the opposite conclusion to *Lang*, above, with facts that are remarkably similar. The case is *Arden B. Engerbretsen et. al v. Arden A. Engerbretsen, et al.*, 675 A.2d 13 (Delaware 1995). Arden B. Engerbretsen and his wife were insured by United Services Auto Association (USAA) under homeowners and personal umbrella policies. Their son, Arden A Engerbretsen, his wife, and their two children were staying with them while he looked for employment. They arrived there in March of 1990 and intended to leave by November 5th, either for a hoped-for job in New York or to move to Arizona.

However, on November 2, 1990, Arden A. Engerbretsen was using a tractor-mower owned by his parents (Arden B.) to mow the lawn behind their house. Unbeknownst to him, his son Andrew, age 2, was nearby. He backed the mower and accidentally knocked Andrew down and ran over him. A claim was submitted, and USAA extended coverage under the homeowners section F medical payments to others. The insurer denied coverage under the liability portion, however, citing the exclusion of coverage for bodily injury to an insured. (USAA later asserted that payment under medical payments did not consitute a waiver of the exclusionary provision of coverage E liability.)

The superior court considered the meaning of "residents of the [named insured's] household" since this term was not defined in the homeowners policy. "The main disagreement among the courts relates to whether, in determining the meaning of the term, the subjective intentions of the occupier and the policyholder as to the transient or permanent nature of the stay should be considered. In other words, the dispute involves whether the temporal element of the stay at the policyholder's premises is relevant to the analysis," stated the court, noting that both plaintiffs and defendants brought several cases to prove their point.

One of the cases pointed to by the defendants (Arden A.) was *Lang*, discussed above. As noted earlier, the two cases are remarkably similar. But the court in *Engerbretsen*, although noting the similarity, said "there are other factors to consider which may overcome the stated intent of a transitory living arrangement... The circumstances in this case go beyond a mere temporary living arrangement while the father looked for employment... In the court's view, the record establishes a portrait of a close, extended family, living as members of a single household under one roof for a substantial period of time, sharing meals and vacationing together. The court is convinced that the circumstances in this case... outweigh the declared subjective intention of defendants of a temporary living arrangement. Thus, the court concludes that defendants were residents of the grandparents' household under the policy on the date of Andrew's accident." Therefore, the court held the defendants were residents and so fell within the injury to an insured exclusion of coverage E. Coverage was precluded. It should be noted that the question of whether USAA's payment under coverage F medical payments to others constituted a waiver of their right to deny coverage under coverage E was not addressed.

Agent Tip

Whenever there is a doubt or question as to who will be considered a resident relative for coverage (or exclusionary) purposes, it may be prudent to review case law in any given jurisdiction.

Chapter 4

Motor Vehicles

Introduction

The fact that there is no agreement among umbrella insurers as to what exactly a "motor vehicle" is means that anyone wishing to determine whether coverage is provided or excluded must carefully read the form. First, check the definition to see what any given insurer considers a "motor vehicle." Then consider "who is an insured" for use of a particular vehicle. Finally, examine the exclusions. This chapter primarily looks at coverage for motor vehicles; particularly, private passenger motor vehicles. Recreational motor vehicles will be discussed in Chapter 5.

The "Family Auto"

Because the reason many persons purchase a personal umbrella is to provide increased liability protection for damages arising from covered auto accidents, it is important to understand exactly who is an insured for use of the family's private passenger auto(s). As noted earlier, the ISO personal auto policy (PAP), 1998 edition, extends coverage in event a spouse ceases to be a resident of the household for a period of the earlier of: (a) the end of 90 days following the spouse's change of residency; (b) the effective date of another policy listing the spouse as a named insured; or (c) the end of the policy period. Therefore, the spouse continues to be a named insured during this time, and so covered on the auto policy. However, there is currently no such provision in any of the umbrella forms reviewed.

Agent Tip

Therefore, if this situation arises, contact the insurer to see if arrangement can be made to extend the umbrella coverage similarly until other coverage can be arranged.

Family Members

A personal umbrella should cover the named insured, spouse (if resident of the same household), and family members or resident relatives as defined. It is not uncommon for young persons, with their parents' consent, to have vehicles titled in their own names. Technically, these vehicles should be written on separate policies, since at that point for physical damages purposes the parents are presumed to have no insurable interest. Some insurers, however, will allow the vehicles to be added to the parents' policy.

Agent Tip

If family members have their own auto policies, it is vital that the limits of coverage be in accordance with the umbrella insurer's requirements. The family members and their autos should be shown as insureds on an application or declarations.

Problems can arise, though, if the policy language conveys that only autos owned by the named insured (or "you") are covered. (Note: unless otherwise indicated, assume that "motor vehicle" refers to a "family-type" auto, pick-up, or van.) For example:

We do not provide coverage for:

1. Anyone except you for accidents involving a motor vehicle which any other covered person [relatives who reside with the named insured]:

   (a) owns.

   (b) rents.

   (c) has supplied for his regular use.

   (d) has as a temporary substitute and which is not shown on the declarations.

It would seem that the intent is either to preclude coverage (except for "you") for owned or regularly furnished vehicles not shown on the declarations (therefore avoiding providing free insurance), or to follow the ISO personal auto policy (see "Company Cars," below.) But the language is unclear. "You" means the named insured and spouse; if a vehicle is titled to the 18-year old son, is coverage for him precluded even though the vehicle is shown on the declarations? Note that the words "and which is not shown on the declarations" refer only to a temporary substitute by virtue of the placement of the phrase. There are ways to insure regularly furnished vehicles and still meet umbrella requirements, which will be discussed in the "Company Car" section below.

Agent Tip

If confronted with this language, request written underwriting clarification of intent, and ask as well that written clarification be given to the claims department. Remember, though, that written clarification is not part of the contract.

Ambiguity can be avoided, however, through language such as:

> This policy does not apply to...any liability arising out of the maintenance or use, including loading or unloading, of any non-owned motor vehicle regularly used or available for use by you or any member of your household, if the motor vehicle is not covered by an underlying policy.

The personal umbrella language should clearly state that the named insured, spouse, and family members are covered for use of a motor vehicle. "Use" of a motor vehicle is rarely defined, and it should be noted that "use" need not equate with actual operation of the vehicle. For example, a passenger may be "using" a vehicle to provide personal transportation. The passenger could distract the driver, thus causing an accident. An owner may ask a neighbor to run an errand for him; even though not actually driving he is still "using" the car. Therefore, the insuring language should address these situations. See, for example, below:

> "Insured" means you and also:
>
> a. any member of your household [defined as related by blood, marriage, or adoption or a ward or foster child whose principal place of residence is the same as the named insured's]. But with respect to motor vehicles to which this policy applies, a member of your household is covered only as follows:
>
> (1) while using a motor vehicle owned by you or any member of your household;
>
> (2) while using a motor vehicle not owned by you or any member of your household provided such use is with the reasonable belief that the person using it is entitled to do so.

Similarly:

"Insured" means:

1. You.

2. A "family member."

3. Any person using an "auto", "recreational motor vehicle" [such as a golf cart or snowmobile], or watercraft, which is owned by you and covered under this policy. Any person using a temporary substitute for such "auto" or "recreational motor vehicle" is also an "insured."

This latter provision of coverage for "any person" is bounded by an exclusion for any person using an "auto", "recreational motor vehicle", or watercraft without a reasonable belief that that person is entitled to do so. Limiting such coverage to a permissive user prevents, say, a car thief from claiming coverage under an insured's personal umbrella policy. The *permissive user provision* is discussed in greater detail below.

Organizations

In keeping with the wording of the ISO personal auto policy (PAP), most personal umbrella forms cover persons or organizations with respect to legal responsibility for acts or omissions of an insured. So, for example, an insured may be using her car to help deliver Girl Scout cookies. If she negligently runs into another vehicle at an intersection and the other driver sues both the insured and the Girl Scout Council, the Council is an insured. An "organization" need not be not for profit; it may be a business, which, if legally responsible for an insured's use of an auto, is also an insured.

The policy language to look for to see if an organization is also an insured will be something like:

"Insured" means:

4. Any other person or organization but only with respect to the legal responsibility for acts or omissions of you or any "family member" while you or any "family member" is using an "auto" ... covered under this policy...

Similarly:

> We'll [the insurer] also cover any person or organization legally responsible for the use of an automobile, if it's used by you or with your permission. But the use has to be for the intended purpose.

Note that, in the above provision, the insurer stipulates that usage must be " for the intended purpose." Probably the intention is to prevent an organization's claiming coverage on shaky grounds. For example, if an insured uses his auto in the course of committing a criminal act, presumably this is not the purpose "intended" by the organization (although the insured may certainly intend the purpose!) and so the organization will not be an insured for coverage purposes.

However, there are two things to be aware of regarding this coverage provision. First, in these examples, no matter how many persons or organizations seek coverage for a claim arising out of one occurrence, the limits will not be increased. Second, not all auto policies — particularly the non-standard ones — cover anyone other than the named insured. Many umbrella insurers, for this reason among others, are hesitant to write an umbrella policy over a non-standard auto policy.

Agent Tip

If this coverage provision is important — if an insured, say, does much driving for a charitable organization, or even occasionally drives the charity's clients — then consider increasing the umbrella limits. Remember, limits are not increased, no matter how many claims arise out of an occurrence. It might also be prudent to see how the charity's own insurance would respond to the volunteer's use of his vehicle.

Legal Representatives

There is another class of insured with regards to motor vehicles, and that is the insured's legal representative(s). This provision appears in different places depending upon the umbrella form reviewed; sometimes under "who is an insured" and other times in the conditions or general provisions. One form not only covers legal representatives, but also persons acting as such until a legal representative is appointed:

> Each of the following is also an insured:
>
> a. A person or an organization having proper temporary custody of your property if you die, but only:

(1) With respect to liability due to the maintenance or use of that property; and

(2) Until your legal representative has been appointed.

b. Your legal representative if you die, but only with respect to duties as such. That representative will have all of your rights and all of your duties under this endorsement.

This provision of coverage for a legal representative is found in the general provisions under "transfer of your interest in this policy":

1. Your rights and duties under this policy may not be assigned without our written consent. However, if you die, coverage will be provided for:

c. The legal representative of the deceased person as if a named insured shown in the declarations. This applies only with respect to the representative's legal responsibility to maintain or use your "autos" or premises covered under this policy.

In event of the insured's death, legal representatives become insureds, but only with respect to liability arising out of their duties. So, for example, the legal representative could not claim to be an insured under a deceased's umbrella if she negligently causes an accident while driving her own car for her own personal business.

Permissive Users

Questions of what constitutes permission are often vexatious. The ISO personal auto policy (1994 edition) excludes liability coverage for "using a vehicle without a reasonable belief that that `insured' is entitled to do so" (exclusion A.8.), and yet the liability insuring agreement (B.1.) considers that "◊`Insured' as used in this part means you or any `family member' for the ownership, maintenance or use of any auto or `trailer.'◊"

In the case of *United Services Automobile Association v. William Todd Dunn et al.*, 598 So. 2d 1169 (Louisiana 1992), this language led to the appellate court's holding that the language was ambiguous, and so resolved the suit in favor of the insured. James Timothy, a resident of his parents' household, allegedly struck two pedestrians. The auto and umbrella insurer, USAA, denied coverage, asserting that the young driver did not have his parents' permission to drive when the accident occurred. Everyone involved — pedestrians, driver, and insurer — filed suit for summary judgment.

The insurer held that the policy clearly and unambiguously excluded coverage for all persons using the covered auto without the named insured's consent. The trial court disagreed, and the appellate court, construing language like that above, affirmed that the ambiguity led to coverage. Stated the court, "When the coverage clause and the exclusion are read together, we see that coverage is provided to family members and to any person who uses a covered auto, except for any person who uses a covered auto who does not have a reasonable belief that he or she is entitled to use it. If the company had intended to exclude family members, it should have used the term 'covered person' in the exclusion because 'covered person' was defined to mean family members and any persons using covered autos. Because the exclusion does not apply to family members, coverage is afforded to family member James G. Timothy."

The current ISO personal auto policy (PAP) has eliminated potential confusion by excepting "family members" using "your covered auto" from exclusion A.8. However, there are forms that are not clear as to coverage for family members or permissive users.

For example, is it only the named insured who can give permission to another to use covered vehicles? The following language suggests that this is indeed the case:

> Covered person means:
>
> 1. anyone using your motor vehicles or equipment with your permission who is covered under one of your basic policies.

Similarly:

> For occurrences caused by the use of automobiles...we'll also cover anyone else who uses your automobile with your permission provided it's used for the purpose you intended.

On prom night a teenager borrows his father's Lincoln to drive his date to the dance. While at the prom, he and some friends consume some alcohol. However, the teenager recognizes that he should not drive, and asks his date (who is a licensed driver — let's not muddy the waters!) to drive him home. While on the way, she negligently hits the gas instead of the brake, and runs into another vehicle at a stop sign, seriously injuring the other driver and passenger. Is there coverage for the date under the above umbrella form? Is the date a "permissive user"?

A Mississippi case is instructive. The facts are these: The insured bought a new car for his daughter in anticipation of her receiving her driver's license. The car was titled to his company and added to his business auto and umbrella policies. (He did this with all his family's vehicles. This is not an uncommon practice.) Christi, the daughter, was given permission to drive the car to school and to school functions. If she wanted to drive anywhere else, she was to ask permission. Three months later, Christi was given permission to take the car, and drove some friends around town, stopping at a gas station. A friend (Corey) asked if he could drive the car, and upon Christi's giving him permission, took off with another friend, Rodney. Meanwhile, Christi got into another car and left the gas station.

Corey flipped the car, and Rodney was killed. Corey was insured under a State Farm policy with $50,000 limits. Christi's father's insurer tentatively offered a $100,000, and then a $200,000 settlement, but then rescinded the offer. Rodney's mother sued Corey, Christi's parents, and the father's business. Coverage turned upon whether Corey was an insured under the business auto omnibus clause — "anyone else while using with your permission a covered auto..." A similar clause was contained in the umbrella.

All parties agreed that for Corey to be an insured he must have Christi's father's express or implied permission. In *Federated Mutual Insurance Company v. Corey Davis et al.*, 919 F.Supp. 1001 (Mississippi 1995), the district court looked to the Mississippi supreme court's past resolution of issues relating to the coverage of a permissive user, and found no reason to deviate. The supreme court held that "The `general rule' that a permittee may not allow a third party to `use' the named insured's car has generally been held not to preclude recovery under the omnibus clause where (1) the original permittee is riding in the car at the time of the accident, or (2) the second permittee, in using the vehicle is serving some purpose of the original permittee. The courts generally reason that under such circumstances the second permittee is `operating' the car for the `use of the first permittee' and that such `use' is within the coverage of the omnibus clause." Having looked to this "general rule" it did no good for Corey Davis to argue that his purpose in driving Christi's vehicle was to prevent it standing unattended in the gas station lot. There was no coverage under the Federated policy. (It should also be noted that Corey Davis held that Federated, having once made a settlement offer, should be estopped from denying coverage. The court disagreed, saying that waiver and estoppel could not be used to extend coverage or create primary liability where none existed.)

This case's outcome is instructive in the situation of the prom date. It could be argued that the date was serving the father's purpose by bringing his son home. Therefore, there would be coverage.

Federated is useful for another reason. The court also considered another situation, and that is when a parent purchases a car for his son or daughter, but "turns the car over to" the young driver. In the case of *State Farm Mutual Automobile Insurance Co. v. Moore*, 289 So. 3d 909 (Mississippi 1974), even though the father had told his son not to let anyone else drive his car, by giving his son unrestricted use of the vehicle (the son had the only set of keys) the son had "broad, unfettered domination" of the car and, when he as first permittee gave permission to a friend to drive him, the friend, or second permittee, was covered.

Agent Tip

Review any restrictions to coverage carefully with clients, particularly those with young drivers. The only thing necessary to realize that young people have no qualms about driving their friends' cars is to watch a sixteen year old boy's eyes light up when someone pulls into the school lot in a new red Mustang convertible!

Corporate Vehicles and Business Use

There are several considerations in regards to corporate vehicles. This next section looks at personal umbrella coverage for "company cars," corporately titled vehicles, and business use.

Company Cars

A common situation in many households is for one person to have a company car; that is, a vehicle regularly furnished for his use in connection with a business. (Situations where a business owner titles the family's personal passenger vehicles in the name of the business are considered separately; see below.) Often, the company car may be used for personal needs as well as for the business. The personal auto policy (PAP) does not provide liability coverage for an insured's use of any vehicle furnished or available for the named insured's regular use (exclusion B.2.). Therefore, if an insured has a regularly-furnished vehicle, care must be taken in determining how any given personal umbrella will treat this exposure.

Some forms address this exposure directly:

> We do not provide coverage for anyone except you and your relatives living with you for a motor vehicle covered under a commercial or business automobile policy shown on our declarations as one of your basic policies.

Similarly:

> This policy does not apply to any liability arising out of the maintenance or use, including loading or unloading, of any non-owned motor vehicle regularly used or available for use by you or any member of your household, if the motor vehicle is not covered by an underlying policy.

These forms indicate that the personal umbrella will respond provided there are adequate underlying limits. In the first example above the underlying policy must be indicated on the declarations for coverage to apply. Note as well that, in the first example, only the named insured and resident relatives will be afforded umbrella coverage. The business will not be given 'insured' status.

Agent Tip

Sometimes an umbrella insurer will not write an umbrella over an auto exposure it does not insure. In other cases, the umbrella insurer will consider an umbrella if it writes the commercial auto account. Each case is different. If a client has a company car, review underlying policies carefully and check with the personal umbrella underwriter to see how this exposure should be handled.

Coverage gaps can arise, though, where the only auto in a household is a company-furnished vehicle and there is no personal auto policy in place. Or, there may be personal autos along with the business auto. Depending on the particular business auto policy in place, the company-car insured may not be covered for his or her use of any other vehicle. The ISO personal auto policy, remember, precludes liability coverage:

> We do not provide liability coverage for the ownership, maintenance or use of:
>
> 2. Any vehicle, other than 'your covered auto', which is:
>
>   a. Owned by you; or
>
>   b. Furnished or available for your regular use.
>
> 3. Any vehicle, other than 'your covered auto', which is:
>
>   a. Owned by any 'family member'; or
>
>   b. Furnished or available for the regular use of any 'family member'.

> However, this exclusion (B.3.) does not apply to you while you are maintaining or 'occupying' any vehicle which is;
>
> a. Owned by a 'family member'; or
>
> b. Furnished or available for the regular use of a 'family member'.

Say, for example, husband and wife are both named insureds on a PAP. The wife has a company car. One day the husband's personal car is in the shop for repairs, but since his wife is out of town he takes the company car. While using his cell phone to call a customer he glances down at some papers, and negligently runs into the back of a legally stopped school bus. The family's personal auto policy will respond to this loss, since exclusion 3.b. does not apply to 'you' — the named insured — while occupying a vehicle regularly furnished to a family member. But what if a son drives a company car, and the daughter drives it and causes an accident? She is not 'you'. Or, perhaps the couple resides in New York City where they have no need for a personal car, relying on a company car for transportation, or renting a vehicle if they travel.

There are ways to plug these coverage gaps. First, in the case of a regularly furnished company car where there are personal vehicles, ISO extended non-owned coverage for named individuals PP 03 06 may be attached to the personal auto policy. All family members that should be covered must be listed. The endorsement deletes exclusions B.2. and B.3., so that family members other than "you" driving a company car are covered. (The endorsement also responds to the insured's personal use of a company car.) Or perhaps there is no personal car in the household, but auto coverage is an umbrella requirement. A named non-owner policy should be considered. If using the ISO forms, it is endorsement PP 03 22. Exclusions B.2. and B.3 are amended so that the references to "regularly furnished" are deleted, so personal use of a company vehicle is covered.

Agent Tip

Caution! If using the named non-owner form, then each family member who should be covered must be named on the endorsement. There is no (repeat, *no*) automatic coverage for a resident spouse or other family members.

Family Autos Titled to a Business

A common way for a business owner to shift risk away from personal assets is to title the family vehicles in the name of the business. Therefore, in regards to a personal umbrella, there is no underlying personal auto policy in place unless one of two things happens. For one, a named non-owner policy may be purchased. Two, the business auto policy may be endorsed to provide coverage. Remember, the personal umbrella provides broad coverage that is designed to cover the insured's use of any covered vehicle. A business auto policy, unless so written or endorsed, will not automatically cover an insured's use of a borrowed or rented car. (Of course, symbol 1 is "any auto," and that includes owned and non-owned vehicles.)

A business auto policy may be endorsed by adding drive other car coverage — broadened coverage for named individuals CA 99 10 or individual named insured CA 99 17. If the CA 99 10 is used, care must be taken that family members other than the spouse (who is automatically covered) are named; otherwise they will not be considered insureds. If the CA 99 17 is added, then family members of the named insured are considered insureds for any covered auto of the private passenger type and owned by the named insured. They are also insureds for the use of non owned autos (certain restrictions apply; see the endorsement. See also *Business Auto Coverage Guide,* National Underwriter Co., 1998 for more information.)

Business Use

Generally, the coverage (or exclusion) for a vehicle used in business is similar to that found in the personal auto policy (PAP). For example:

> This policy does not apply to:
>
> 1. Any liability arising out of:
>
>   a. any business pursuits or business property of any insured, except for:
>
>   (1) the business use of a private passenger automobile or owned watercraft, unless used to carry persons or property for a charge.

Similarly:

> As you would expect... the following [are not] covered:
>
> 1. We will not cover personal injury or property damage arising out of business or business property unless covered under one or more of the basic policies. We will, however, cover you or a relative for business use of a private passenger car as long as it is not used as a taxi or for hire...

Therefore, the insured's use of his personal vehicle to make sales calls is covered.

Sometimes the lines between business and non business usage become blurred so that a court makes the call. In the case of *Industrial Indemnity Company v. Peter Vukmarkovic et al.*, 562 N.E.2d 1073 (Illinois 1990), the lines became very blurred indeed. Charles Latimer, an owner of Woodfield Ford, purchased a limousine. He then entered into an agreement with Lisle Livery, Inc., under which Lisle had complete control and maintenance of the vehicle in exchange for proceeds from their use of the vehicle in their livery business. Charles Latimer had an auto dealers' policy, which also provided a personal umbrella liability extension.

The umbrella liability extension provided coverage for "any person using an auto owned by ...the named insured...with the named insured's permission." The liability extension excluded " any business or business pursuits of an insured or to property on which a business is conducted by an insured..."

Lisle Livery assigned Peter Vukmarkovic to drive the limousine. He parked the vehicle at his home, and was permitted to use it for his own errands when not working as a driver. On the night in question, he picked up some passengers at the airport and drove them to their requested location. He then went to a late dinner and to a night club with some friends. On the way home in the early morning hours, he struck and severely injured a pedestrian.

The resulting suit named Vukmarkovic, Latimer, and Lisle Livery. The complaint was dropped against Latimer and Lisle, however. Lisle Livery's policy paid its limits, but the injured pedestrian attempted to collect on his judgment against Vukmarkovic by instituting a garnishment action to collect under the Industrial policy, based on Vukmarkovic's status as an insured.

The court had to look at the two umbrella provisions noted above, that for a permissive user, and the business pursuits exclusion. The insurer did not dispute that Vukmarkovic was a permissive user, but held that the "business pursuits" exclusion precluded coverage in the first place. The appellate court found otherwise. The court said that Vukmarkovic was driving the vehicle for purely personal reasons at the time of the accident. The insurer argued that Latimer's purchase and transfer of the limousine to Lisle was a business activity. But the court said it was not clear that the arrangement was part of Latimer's "trade, profession, or occupation"; but was more in the nature of a passive investment. Further, the use to which the vehicle was put at the time of the accident was the deciding factor, and since the usage was personal, there was coverage.

Foreign Travel

Personal umbrella policies respond to covered occurrences anywhere in the world. This includes auto accidents. Indeed, a reason to purchase an umbrella policy has traditionally been its providing primary coverage for accidents occurring outside the United States, its territories and possessions, Canada, or Puerto Rico. Some umbrella insurers, however, are eliminating this coverage, and require the insured to carry underlying auto insurance limits which may be at least as high as those normally required for umbrella coverage. Failure to do so results in the umbrella's responding to a covered loss as if the required coverage had been in place. In other words, the umbrella will not drop down to fill in the coverage gap.

Agent Tip

If any of your clients rent vehicles abroad, then check the umbrella policy in advance to alert them as to what is required.

Chapter 5

Recreational Motor Vehicles and other Fun Stuff

Introduction

In contrast with the coverages and exclusions for the use of autos, in the case of recreational motor vehicles umbrella forms have little in common with each other. For example, one form will not, under any circumstances, respond to use of any aircraft, even if covered under the named insured's basic policy. Another form provides coverage if the aircraft is chartered with crew by or on behalf of the named insured. Most forms stress that there must be underlying coverage in place for recreational motor vehicles, but one form does not address the issue at all except for mopeds, mini bikes, and the like.

When it comes to air- and watercraft, there is little need for definitions. Except for noting that, for exclusionary purposes, hobby or model aircraft are excepted, there is general agreement as to what air- and watercraft are. (The ISO homeowners 2000 forms, however, have added definitions for aircraft, hovercraft, watercraft, and motor vehicles.) But there is difficulty in interpreting coverage for recreational motor vehicles simply because of the variety in definitions. One form defines "recreational vehicles" in such a way that the reader is left to surmise that the definition apples to *motorized* vehicles; another form does not really define such vehicles at all. The following section discusses various definitions (and sometimes lack thereof) for these conveyances — motorized vehicles that are not required to be licensed for road use.

Motorized Recreational Vehicles

Virtually all umbrellas contain some definition of a recreational motor vehicle. In the various forms reviewed, there were two that did not specifically define them. One excluded coverage for mopeds, motor scooters, motorized bicycles licensed for road use or subject to financial responsibility laws (which some insurers consider recreational motor vehicles). The other form simply lumps all "motorized vehicles" together:

> Motorized vehicle means a self-propelled land or amphibious vehicle regardless of method of surface contact. This does not include vehicles that are designed and used to assist the handicapped and are not required to be licensed for road use.

This is not to say, however, that there is automatic coverage for such conveyances as snowmobiles and all-terrain vehicles. It may be that the application for umbrella insurance outlines the underlying coverage requirements and gives examples; sometimes the conditions contain the information. In other instances, coverage is excluded except to the extent that coverage is provided by underlying insurance.

Definitions

When reviewing the definitions below, keep in mind that both Insurance Services Office (ISO) and American Association of Insurance Services (AAIS) homeowners forms provide limited coverage for certain recreational motor vehicles. When additional coverage is required, many persons purchase separate policies, or endorse the coverage onto a homeowners or auto policy (as for a golf cart or snowmobile). Practices vary from insurer to insurer. It is important, therefore, to make sure the umbrella definitions and coverages are no more limited than those in underlying policies. Neither the 1991 nor the 2000 ISO homeowners forms contain a specific definition of a recreational motor vehicle, but, the exclusion (discussed below) in the 1991 form references "a motorized land conveyance designed for recreational use off public roads, not subject to motor vehicle registration...." (The 2000 form is slightly different, as will be seen below.) In contrast, the AAIS homeowners definition is:

> "Recreational motor vehicle" means a 'motorized vehicle', a trailer, or attached equipment that is designed or is used for leisure time activities, and which is not a 'motor vehicle' [which is a vehicle subject to registration or designed to be used on public roads]."
>
> "Motorized vehicle" means a self-propelled land or amphibious vehicle regardless of method of surface contact.
>
> This does not include vehicles that are designed and used to assist the handicapped and are not required to be licensed for road use. [The definition of "motorized vehicle" is identical to that found in the AAIS umbrella.]

Note that in the AAIS definition a recreational motor vehicle may be one that is amphibious. This closes a potential loophole in the 1991 ISO definition, which refers strictly to land conveyances. The ISO homeowners 2000 forms, however, have redefined a "motor vehicle" so that this loophole is closed:

"Motor vehicle" means:

a. A self-propelled land or amphibious vehicle; or

b. Any trailer or semitrailer which is being carried on, towed by or hitched for towing by a vehicle described in a. above.

As will be seen below, one umbrella form includes an "amphibious" vehicle in its definition.

A common umbrella definition of a recreational motor vehicle is:

"Recreational motor vehicle" means:

1. All-terrain vehicle;

2. Dune buggy;

3. Golf cart;

4. Snowmobile; or

5. Any other motorized land vehicle which is designed for recreational use off public roads.

Although the above definition appears all-encompassing (for example, 'any' motorized land vehicle includes, say, a dirt bike), questions could well arise that would have to be settled in a court of law. Where does an amphibious vehicle fit in this definition? Is it a 'land' vehicle? Or does its ability to go into water make it a watercraft? The legal principle of *ejusdem generis* holds that, "where general words follow an enumeration of persons or things, by words of a particular and specific meaning, such general words are not to be construed in their widest extent, but are to be held as applying only to persons or things of the same general kind or class as those specifically mentioned." (See *Black's Law Dictionary, Fifth Edition.*) In accordance with this principle, an amphibious vehicle is outside the definition. Since few persons possess such a vehicle, there is not a great need to belabor the point. However, this does make clear the need for care in comparing forms.

The umbrella form that addresses the variety of recreational motor vehicles, including an amphibious vehicle, states:

> "Recreational motor vehicle" means a recreational land motor vehicle designed for use off public roads. This includes a motorized all terrain vehicle, amphibious vehicle, dune buggy, golfmobile, snowmobile, trailbike, or mini bike.

Language in an umbrella policy — indeed, in any contract — is important because it forms the basis of the agreement between the entity drawing up the contract, and the other party to the contract. In the most common underlying policies, that is, homeowners and auto policies, the language has been tested through challenge in court. But there has been little judicial interpretation regarding umbrella policies.

For this reason words and terms used in umbrella policies should either be defined, or, at the very least, not open to differing opinions as to meaning. Judges typically resolve ambiguous contract language — wherein reasonable persons disagree as to meaning — in favor of the insured. Take, for example, the following:

> We won't pay liability for any accident related to the ownership, care or use of a motorcycle, 'snowmobile' or recreational vehicle unless the accident is covered by 'your underlying insurance'.

"Recreational vehicle" is not defined, and it appears from the context that the insurer has equated "recreational vehicle" with a motorized recreational vehicle (which would accord with *ejusdem generis*). But according to *Webster's Collegiate Dictionary, Tenth Edition,* the first definition of a vehicle is "carriage, conveyance." The fourth definition is "a means of carrying or transporting something; conveyance as a: motor vehicle [or] b: a piece of mechanized equipment. By definition, then, a child's wagon is thus a vehicle, and one used for recreation. Remember, courts generally turn first to a common desktop dictionary if a questionable, undefined word or phrase is used in a contract.

The difficulty this lapse in precision leads to is demonstrated in this exclusion:

> We will not cover personal injury or property damage arising out of the ownership, maintenance, use, loading, or unloading of an automobile, watercraft, or recreational vehicle while practicing for or participating in any prearranged or organized racing, speed, demolition or stunting contest or activity...

Mountain bikers beware! According to the above exclusion, bodily injury and property damage arising out of racing activity — even a 100 mile bike road race for a favorite charity — may not be covered.

Although most of the above definitions hold a "recreational motor vehicle" to be one designed for off-the-road usage, the definition below is much more encompassing:

> "Recreational Vehicle" means:
>
> A. motorcycles, motor scooters, mopeds, and motorized bicycles, including any similar two or three wheeled vehicles designed or licensed for use on public roads; or
>
> B. all-terrain vehicles, golf carts, trail or dirt bikes, mini bikes, snowmobiles, and dune buggies, including similar vehicles designed for use on or off public roads.

In summation, should there be any question as to what an insurer means, it is far better to obtain clarification beforehand than to allow a court of law to make the determination.

Coverage under the Homeowners Forms

Before discussing who is an insured for recreational vehicle coverage purposes, the wisest place to begin is to look at the liability coverage for such vehicles provided by the homeowners forms. First, the AAIS (Edition 2.0):

> "Motorized vehicles" [self propelled land or amphibious vehicle] — We pay for the bodily injury or the property damage which:
>
> a. occurs on the insured premises and is a result of the ownership, maintenance, use, loading, or unloading of:
>
> (1) a motorized vehicle if it is not subject to "motor vehicle" registration because of its type or use; or
>
> (2) a recreational motor vehicle [a motorized vehicle not subject to motor vehicle registration].
>
> b. results from:
>
> (1) a golf cart while used for golfing purposes;

(2) a utility, boat, camp, or mobile home trailer. However, this coverage does not apply to bodily injury or property damage resulting from a trailer which:

a) is carried on, towed by, or attached to a motor vehicle [designed for use on public roads and subject to motor vehicle registration] or a recreational motor vehicle; or

b) becomes detached while being carried on or towed by a motor vehicle or a recreational motor vehicle; or

(3) a motorized vehicle which is designed only for use off public roads and which is used mainly to service the insured premises. However, this coverage does not apply to bodily injury or property damage which results from a motorized vehicle owned by an insured while used for recreational purposes away from the insured premises, other than a golf cart while used for golfing purposes.

c. results from an insured's use of a recreational motor vehicle which is not owned by an insured.

Immediately apparent is the fact that, unlike the ISO homeowners forms, the AAIS form states both what is and what is not covered. Bodily injury or property damage that occurs on the insured's premises and results from the ownership, maintenance, or use of a recreational motor vehicle is covered. Injury or damage resulting from use of a golf cart for golfing purposes is covered. Injury or damage resulting from use of a nonowned recreational motor vehicle is covered.

Homeowners forms usually do not provide liability coverage for damage to property in the care of an insured, except for property damage caused by fire, smoke, or explosion, sometimes referred to as fire legal liability. (Note, personal property of others used by or in the care of an insured is covered under section I property coverage. But there is no section I property coverage for motor vehicles other than those used to service the premises or assist the handicapped.) There *is* liability coverage, however, under the AAIS form (limited to $500) for damage an insured causes to a nonowned recreational vehicle:

> ...property damage to motorized vehicles not subject to motor vehicle registration and not owned by an insured if the motorized vehicle is used only to service the premises or if it is designed for recreational use off public roads.

Therefore, if an insured borrows a friend's snowmobile and plows into a tree, totalling the snowmobile, $500 is available to pay for the damage to the snowmobile under the incidental liability coverages.

The ISO form (1991 edition) takes a different approach to reach the same level of coverage:

> Coverage E - Personal Liability and Coverage F - Medical Payments to Others do not apply to bodily injury or property damage... arising out of:
>
> 1. The ownership, maintenance, use, loading or unloading of motor vehicles or all other motorized land conveyances, including trailers, owned or operated by or rented or loaned to an insured;
> 2. The entrustment by an insured of a motor vehicle or any other motorized land conveyance to any person; or
> 3. Vicarious liability, whether or not statutorily imposed, for the actions of a child or minor using a conveyance excluded in paragraph 1. or 2. above.
>
> This exclusion does not apply to:
>
> 1. A trailer not towed by or carried on a motorized land conveyance.
> 2. A motorized land conveyance designed for recreational use off public roads, not subject to motor vehicle registration and:
>   (a) Not owned by an insured; or
>   (b) Owned by an insured and on an insured location;
> 3. A motorized golf cart when used to play golf on a golf course....

The ISO homeowners 2000 forms follow a slightly different format. The definitions section contains the following, which then refer to the section II liability exclusions:

> ...In addition, certain words and phrases are defined as follows:
>
> 1. "Aircraft Liability", "Hovercraft Liability", "Motor Vehicle Liability" and "Watercraft Liability" ... mean the following:
>   (a) Liability for bodily injury or property damage arising out of the:

(1) Ownership of such vehicle or craft by an insured;

(2) Maintenance, occupancy, operation, use, loading or unloading of such vehicle or craft by any person;

(3) Entrustment of such vehicle or craft by an insured to any person;

(4) Failure to supervise or negligent supervision of any person involving such vehicle or craft by an insured; and

(5) Vicarious liability, whether or not imposed by law, for the actions of a child or minor involving such vehicle or craft.

Simply put, bodily injury or property damage, except to an insured or to an insured's property, arising out of a recreational vehicle on the insured premises is covered. Bodily injury or property damage arising out of a nonowned motorized recreational vehicle is covered, even if the injury or damage does not occur on the insured's premises. Injury or property damage arising out of the use of a golf cart for golfing purposes is covered. The ISO homeowners 2000 now provides liability coverage for a golf cart used to travel the roads in a private residential community, subject to certain restrictions.

Similar to the AAIS form the ISO form (1991 edition), under the section II additional coverages, provides up to $500 for property damage to property of others:

> [occurring] to a motorized land conveyance designed for recreational use off public roads, not subject to motor vehicle registration and not owned by an insured.

The ISO homeowners 2000 forms increase the coverage to $1000, and change the provision so that it applies to a vehicle that:

(a) is designed for recreational use off public roads;

(b) is not owned by an insured; and

(c) at the time of the occurrence, is not required by law, or regulation issued by a governmental agency, to have been registered for it to be used on public roads or property.

Note the slight but perhaps significant difference. Consider the example above, with one change: the snowmobile is required to be registered with the local forest service to be allowed access to public lands. If the snowmobile has not been so registered and the tree the insured hits is on public property, there is no coverage for the snowmobile.

Obviously, the coverages provided by homeowners policies leave gaps in coverage that must be addressed through other insurance. For example, an insured trailers her snowmobile to a nearby park (that permits such activities) and takes off on a trail. If she causes bodily injury or property damage, her homeowners policy will not respond. Or, an insured, resident of a golf community that has been planned around a golf course, decides to take his golf cart down the public road outside the community to the local grocery store. There is a slight grade down to the store; the cart's brakes fail and the cart crashes into a large plate glass window. Again, no coverage. Since umbrella policies will not drop down to respond to these situations, other underlying coverage must be arranged to be in accordance with umbrella requirements.

Depending upon the insurer, there are ways to cover these exposures. Under the ISO program, liability coverage (as well as coverage for physical damage) for golf carts, dune buggies, ATVs and the like may be endorsed onto the personal auto policy (PAP) by attaching PP 03 23 miscellaneous vehicle endorsement. Liability coverage for snowmobiles may be added by attaching snowmobile endorsement PP 03 20. Physical damage coverage may be included. Under the AAIS program, liability coverage for golf carts used for other than golfing purposes may be endorsed onto the homeowners through endorsement M-432 golf cart liability coverage. (This endorsement also provides physical damage coverage.) Endorsement ML-164 snowmobile liability coverage only may be attached to the homeowners to provide liability coverage for the ownership, maintenance, or use of a snowmobile. (This endorsement does not provide physical damage coverage.)

Who is Insured?

The provisions affording persons and organizations insured status under a personal umbrella for use of a recreational motor vehicle are often similar to those granting coverage for use of an automobile. The named insured and family members as defined are covered for bodily injury or property damage arising out of the use of a recreational motor vehicle, but remember that underlying insurance for such vehicles must be in place, just as with personal automobile insurance. Coverage is no broader for such persons or organizations under the umbrella policy. For example:

"Insured" means:

1. You.

2. A "family member" [a resident relative including a ward, foster child, or person in the care of either the named insured or an insured over age 21].

3. Any person using ...[a] "recreational motor vehicle"... which is owned by you and *covered under this policy* (italics added). Any person using a temporary substitute for [a] "recreational motor vehicle" is also an insured.

4. Any other person or organization but only with respect to the legal responsibility for acts or omissions of you or any "family member" while you or any "family member" is using ... [a] "recreational motor vehicle" covered under this policy. However, the owner or lessor of ... [a] recreational motor vehicle" loaned to or hired for use by an insured or on an insured's behalf, is not an insured.

However, in evaluating coverage for "any person" or for an organization, in many forms it is not altogether clear exactly whom, besides, of course, the named insured and resident relatives, is covered. For example, in the following form:

"Insured" means:

A. you;

B. a relative who resides in your household;

C. a person under the age of 21 and who is in the care of any person included in [A] or [B] above;

D. any person or organization held liable for an act or failure to act by any person included in [A], [B], or [C] above...

This seems clear. Say an insured organizes a day's outing for a local Scout troop on his family's snowmobiles. One of the Scouts is injured, and the insured and the Scout organization are sued. By definition, both are covered. At least, so it would seem. The form that gives the broad definition, above, limits coverage for recreational vehicles, below:

We do not cover damages [bodily injury and property damage] arising out of:

1. the ownership, maintenance, or use of any automobile, boat, or recreational vehicle...

   (a) This exclusion does not apply if the occurrence is covered by required underlying insurance in which case follow form coverage will be provided.

Agent Tip

If confronted with this wording, an agent who knows her clients own recreational vehicles might wish to inquire into their use, and certainly review the underlying policy.

There are instances where the coverage for a permissive user — even a resident relative who might be presumed to have coverage under virtually all circumstances — seems dubious. consider, for example, the following:

> Family member's liability for the use of your hired vehicles or boats without permission. We won't pay the liability of a family member for the use, without permission, of any vehicle or boat that you hire or borrow. This exclusion does not apply to the use of vehicles or boats on real estate you own, rent, or control, or in the roads, paths or other passages next to that real estate.

For a start, whose permission is required? The named insured's or the owner's? What happens when a father and son are out golfing? The father, the named insured, rents a golf cart. He leaves his son, who is 14 (no common sense at that age), and runs into the club house for a moment. The son has never driven a golf cart, and the temptation proves overwhelming. He accidentally runs the cart down a hill, plows into another cart with two people on it, and overturns it, seriously injuring the other golfers. And here is the anomaly. The ISO and AAIS homeowners policies respond, but this umbrella does not. And, in fact, it might be wrong to assume that only motorized private passenger vehicles (autos) are excluded, but the above form does not say this. Rather, the use, without permission, of *any vehicle* is not covered. Without a definition in the form itself, the dictionary definition of "conveyance" prevails.

Motorcycles

For the most, coverage for bodily injury or property damage arising out of the ownership, maintenance or use of motorcycles, mini bikes, and mopeds is excluded under personal umbrella forms unless there is underlying coverage in place. There have been some creative attempts to find underlying coverage in, for example, the homeowners policy, usually through suing for negligent entrustment or negligent supervision. The exclusions for negligent supervision and negligent entrustment, although seemingly alike, are usually construed differently. Negligent entrustment can apply to anyone entrusting a "dangerous instrumentality" to another, while negligent supervision refers to the duty of parents to supervise and control their children. (The current ISO and AAIS forms have since closed this loophole. ISO excludes bodily injury or property damage arising out of the entrustment of a motorized land conveyance; AAIS excludes both entrusting and supervising.)

The case of *Orville Douglass et al. v. Hartford Insurance Company*, 602 F.2d 934 (1979 Colorado), involved a mini bike. Ten-year-old Robert was driving the bike with six-year-old Todd Mahoney as a passenger, apparently looping around the family drive and on to the county road. The bike was struck by a truck. Robert was killed and Todd seriously injured. The insurer refused to defend a possible suit (the statute of limitations would not begin to run until Todd reached the age of majority), citing the exclusion of coverage for "ownership, maintenance, operation, use, loading or unloading" of any recreational motor vehicle away from the premises. But the trial court held, and the appellate court affirmed, that "certainly a mini bike driven by a 10-year-old, with a six-year-old passenger, entering a paved county road, at least invokes the possibility of recovery." Therefore, the insurer was obligated to provide a defense for negligent entrustment.

The appellate court in *Austin Mutual Insurance Company v. Brian D. Klande et al.*, 563 N.W.2d 282 (Minnesota, 1997), reviewed an exclusion for bodily injury or property damage resulting directly or indirectly from "the ownership, operation, maintenance, use, occupancy, renting, loaning, entrusting, supervision, loading, or unloading of motorized vehicles" owned by, operated by, or rented or loaned to, an insured. and held that the exclusion barred coverage. The Klande's son Mitch, an insured on his parents' homeowners' policy, owned an uninsured motorcycle. One day he gave two young visiting relatives rides on the motorcycle, and afterwards parked the cycle in the garage. One of the youngsters, age 9, wandered into the garage, and attempted to mount the cycle. It fell over on him, and the hot muffler severely burned the child. His mother maintained the Klande's homeowners insurer was obligated to indemnify the insureds for the boy's injuries. A denial of coverage led to an action based on negligent supervision.

The court agreed with the insurer. Although it could be possible that two independent acts, one vehicle-related and one not, might combine to cause an injury, in this case the motorcycle was more than just the location of the occurrence. Rather, had the motorcycle not been used for transportation, it would not have become hot. Further, the court held that the motorized vehicle exclusion precluded coverage because the respondents' claim of negligent supervision was not divisible from the ownership and use of the motorcycle itself.

As noted above, coverage for these vehicles is generally excluded unless there is underlying insurance, which will be indicated as the exception to the exclusion. One form, however, does not cover such vehicles at all:

> We do not cover...personal injury or property damage due to the ownership, maintenance, operation, use, loading or unloading of any "motorcycle" [defined as a two or three wheel land motor vehicle designed for use principally on public roads and subject to motor vehicle registration].

Another insurer also essentially excludes such vehicles, but provides an exception:

> This policy does not apply to...any liability arising out of the ownership, maintenance or use, including loading or unloading of:
>
> b. any motorcycle, moped, motor scooter, motorized bicycle or similar vehicle:
>
> (1) licensed for road use; or
>
> (2) subject to the financial responsibility laws of the garaging state.
>
> We will, however, cover any insured while operating a borrowed or rented motorcycle, as long as it is with the owner's permission, used for the purpose intended and not provided for the regular use of any insured...

Agent Tip

If a client has such a vehicle, check the umbrella form carefully. If there are doubts about coverage, check with the underwriter. Some insurers simply do not wish to insure this exposure. If that is the case, it may become necessary to increase the motorcycle policy limits to the maximum possible and recognize that the umbrella will not respond as excess in this case, or to move the account altogether.

Watercraft

Coverage for Watercraft under Homeowners Policies

Both the AAIS and ISO homeowners forms provide limited liability coverage for watercraft. The AAIS form covers bodily injury or property damage:

> ...which results from the maintenance, use, loading, or unloading of:
>
> 1. a watercraft while it is on the insured premises;
>
> 2. a watercraft which is not owned by or rented to an insured if the loss is a result of the activities of an insured [in other words, a borrowed watercraft];
>
> 3. a watercraft which is not owned by an insured and which is powered by inboard or inboard/outboard engines or motors which total 50 horsepower or less [the watercraft can be rented or borrowed];
>
> 4. a sailing vessel with or without auxiliary power which is owned by or is rented to an insured and is less than 26 feet in overall length;
>
> 5. a watercraft which is powered by outboard engines or motors which total 25 horsepower or less; or
>
> 6. a watercraft which is in storage.

Watercraft powered by outboard engines of more than 25 horsepower are covered if listed on the policy; if acquired during the policy period and the insured requests coverage; or if the watercraft is not owned by an insured.

The 1991 ISO homeowners forms do not cover watercraft on the insured's premises (unless of the type covered anyway). While the AAIS form covers borrowed inboard, inboard/outdrive, or outboard watercraft, the ISO form breaks this into rented or borrowed inboard or inboard/outdrive engines of less than 50 horsepower, and borrowed inboard or inboard/outdrive engines of more than 50 horsepower.

The ISO homeowners 2000 forms, as noted earlier, change the format so that "watercraft liability", as defined above, does not apply:

...if, at the time of an occurrence, the involved watercraft is being:

a. Operated in, or practicing for, any prearranged or organized race, speed contest or other competition. This exclusion does not apply to a sailing vessel or a predicted log cruise;

b. Rented to others;

c. Used to carry persons or cargo for a charge; or

d. Used for an business purpose.

The remainder of the watercraft coverages and exclusion remains the same as in the 1991 forms, with the exception that the exclusion of coverage for owned inboard or inboard/outdrive engines includes "those that power a water jet pump," so that watercraft such as jet skis and wet bikes cannot be given broader coverage by arguing that they are not technically inboard-powered craft.

An interesting case arose involving the exclusion of coverage for damages "arising out of the ownership" of any watercraft. The case is *Employers Mutual Liability Insurance Company of Wisconsin v. Michigan Mutual Auto Insurance Company*, 300 N.W.2d 682 (Michigan 1980). The court looked at whether the exclusion applied only when the insured owned a boat at the time of an accident which resulted in damages, or whether it continued to apply when he no longer owned the boat. Arnold Ahonen owned a power boat. He installed a new gas line and filter on the boat, which was insured on a boatowners policy with Wolverine Insurance Company. He had a homeowners policy with Employers Mutual. After he sold the boat, the boatowners policy was cancelled. He then purchased homeowners insurance from Michigan Mutual and an umbrella policy from Employers Mutual.

About a year after the boat was sold, it exploded, injuring six. Ahonen was sued, and all three insurers denied liability. Employers Mutual brought a declaratory judgment action. The appellate court affirmed the trial court's decision, which was that the boatowners policy, by virtue of the transfer of interest, was voided on the sale of the boat. The Employers Mutual homeowners policy did not apply, because the responsibility for the loss accrued at the time the damage occurred rather than at the time of the negligent act, and the policy had been cancelled before the explosion. Finally, since the Michigan Mutual policy did not clearly state that the insured must own the boat at the time of the accident (the explosion), the ambiguity was construed against the insurer.

The umbrella, likewise, could be called on to indemnify if the homeowners limits were not adequate.

Umbrella Watercraft Coverage

There are no standard boatowners forms. Unfortunately, for the insured who has watercraft and wants the extra protection of an umbrella, great care must be taken that coverage given in the one policy is not taken away in the other. Definitions, coverages, and exclusions should each be compatible with the other, lest there be a coverage gap. For example, some boatowners forms do not automatically provide liability coverage for injury arising out of towing a water skier; it must be endorsed. If there is no liability coverage for such activities on an underlying policy, then an umbrella that only gives coverage to the extent that it is provided on an underlying policy will not cover skiing either. And, as previously demonstrated in other chapters, umbrella forms vary significantly in the coverage they provide. This is equally true with regard to watercraft. One form excludes any coverage for watercraft unless there is underlying coverage in place (which may be the coverage provided by a homeowners policy):

> This Personal Umbrella Liability Coverage does not apply to...
>
> .
>
> 4. bodily injury or property damage that results from the ownership, leasing, operation, maintenance, use, occupancy, renting, loaning, entrusting, supervision, loading, or unloading of watercraft. Except as stated in the following paragraph, this exclusion does not apply to the extent that such bodily injury or property damage is covered by underlying insurance at the time of the occurrence.
>
> Regardless of the terms of the underlying insurance, this personal umbrella liability coverage does not apply to bodily injury or property damage that results from the use of watercraft in or in the practice or the preparation for any prearranged or organized racing, speed, or stunt activities or contests. This does not apply to watercraft used in predicted log cruises or to sailing vessels.

This latter exclusion of coverage for bodily injury or property damage arising out of prearranged racing or stunting activities except for log and sail boat racing is common to many boat owners forms, and has made its way into many umbrella forms. The intent is to preclude coverage for activities that warrant specialized coverage. But, since many sail boat owners do, in fact, race (the liability arising out of sail boat races is obviously not the same as that arising out of two jet boats), these activities are covered. Log cruising or log races do not involve speed *per se*, but rather a combination of navigational skill and course plotting. The idea is to arrive at a point at (not before) a certain time, so average speed rather than maximum speed may be critical. Think of a road rally.

Agent Tip

If a client engages in log racing, make sure the umbrella form responds. It is not uncommon for power boats to log race. One form, however, excluded racing events for all boats except for sailboats.

Another form gives broader coverage than that found in, say, the ISO homeowners:

We do not cover.....

8. Personal injury or property damage due to the ownership, maintenance, use, loading or unloading of any watercraft with inboard motor power over 75 (seventy five) horsepower [the ISO homeowners forms do not cover owned inboard-powered watercraft] or over 26 (twenty six) feet or more in overall length owned by, loaned to or rented to an insured. This exclusion does not apply:

   (a) If, on this endorsement's effective date, the watercraft is covered by underlying insurance;

   (b) If we are informed within 30 days after the watercraft is obtained and an additional premium is paid to us; or

   (c) While the watercraft is on premises owned by, rented to or controlled by an insured.

But another umbrella form, granting broad coverage, will:

...cover any insured while operating a borrowed or rented watercraft regardless of size or horsepower, as long as it is with the owner's permission and used for the purpose intended.

Contrast the clarity of the above coverage grant with:

We won't pay the liability of a family member for the use, without permission, of any vehicle or boat that you hire or borrow.

Whose permission must be obtained to circumvent this exclusion? The owner's or the named insured's? If a boat is rented to the named insured, unless the rental agreement specifically states who may operate the watercraft, it is generally understood that family members — insureds — may do so. Further, many boat owners forms are similar to auto policies in that the named insured and resident relatives are insureds for the operation of temporary substitutes. But the above exclusion would appear to disallow coverage unless unspecified permission is first obtained.

Agent Tip

Some insurers do not wish to cover "personal watercraft," which include jet skis and wet bikes. If your client has such a watercraft and wants umbrella coverage, check first with the underwriter before submitting the application.

Airplanes

Rarely do personal umbrella forms provide liability coverage for aircraft, except for model aircraft not designed for carrying persons or cargo. Common exclusions preclude coverage for:

> Bodily injury or property damage arising from:
>
> a. the ownership, maintenance, use, loading or unloading of an aircraft;
>
> b. The entrustment by an insured of an aircraft to any person; or
>
> c. Vicarious liability, whether or not statutorily imposed, for the actions of a child or minor using an aircraft.

And, there are no exceptions. Pity the family that, as a treat, rents a small plane (with a pilot) to fly over the city Christmas lights. If the plane should crash because of, say, a child's actions in distracting the pilot, there would be no coverage. A far-fetched scenario? Yes, of course. But well drafted umbrellas cover the far-fetched as well as the mundane.

Granting coverage in such an instance is this umbrella form:

> We do not cover:
>
> 4. Personal injury or property damage due to the ownership, maintenace, use, loading or unloading of aircraft that is:
>
>   (a) Owned by an insured;
>
>   (b) Chartered without crew by or on behalf of an insured; or
>
>   (c) Not owned by, but furnished for the use of an insured.

Use includes property damage due to the release or discharge of any substance from any aircraft.

Coverage is given here if the insured charters an aircraft with crew, unless the aircraft is used for such activities as, say, crop dusting. Coverage for this activity property belongs under a farm program.

Chapter 6

(Un)Common Exclusions

Introduction

Just as there is no "standard" umbrella form, so there is no consistency with regard to exclusions. In fact, of all the umbrella forms reviewed, there was only one exclusion common to all the forms. Even where one might think to find an exclusion — such as for bodily injury or property damage arising out of business activities — some forms excluded coverage altogether, but others excluded coverage unless underlying coverage was scheduled on the declarations. This chapter first examines exclusions that occur in the majority of the forms reviewed (the common exclusions) and then concludes with a discussion of uncommon exclusions; that is, those that do not appear with any consistency.

Common Exclusions

Workers Compensation

The one exclusion common to all forms applies to workers compensation. There are several variations of the exclusion:

> This policy does not apply to... any liability that is payable or must be provided for under a workers' compensation, occupational disease, unemployment compensation or disability benefits law.

The first exclusion on another umbrella form reads:

> We do not cover... personal injury [defined as mental or bodily injury, sickness, or disease] to a person eligible for payments voluntarily provided by an insured

or required to be provided by the insured under a workers' compensation, nonoccupational disability or occupational disease law.

Remember, homeowners forms do not cover this exposure either. The exclusion in the ISO forms is:

Coverage E — Personal Liability, does not apply to:

d. Bodily injury to any person eligible to receive any benefits:

(1) Voluntarily provided; or

(2) Required to be provided;

by the insured under any:

(1) Workers' compensation law;

(2) Nonoccupational disability law; or

(3) Occupational disease law...

As might be expected, the ISO umbrella form (DL 98 01 06 98) incorporates the identical provisions into exclusion A.17. The same is true of the AAIS homeowners policy and umbrella form (UM 0001 01 00), where the exclusion is:

Coverage L [personal liability] does not apply to... bodily injury to a person, including a domestic employee, if the insured has a workers' compensation policy covering the injury or if benefits are payable or are required to be provided by the insured under a workers' compensation, non-occupational disability, occupational disease, or like law.

War and Nuclear Exclusions

Oddly enough, exclusions of coverage for bodily injury or property damage arising out of war or nuclear action do not appear in every umbrella, even though these exclusions appear in both the AAIS and ISO homeowners forms. One umbrella form excludes

...injury or damage intentionally caused by you, at your direction, or with your knowledge or consent...

and may be relying on this "intentional act" exclusion (which will be discussed in depth below) to eliminate coverage. There is no specific exclusion, however, such as:

> This policy does not apply to... any loss caused directly or indirectly by war, including undeclared war, civil war, insurrection, rebellion, revolution, war-like act by a military force or military personnel, destruction or seizure or use for a military purpose, and including any consequence of any of these. Discharge of a nuclear weapon shall be deemed a warlike act even if accidental.

Another form does not exclude injury or damage arising out of war, but does exclude:

> Personal injury or property damage for which an insured under this endorsement is also an insured under a nuclear energy liability policy or would be an insured but for its termination upon exhaustion of its limits of liability. A nuclear energy liability policy is a policy issued by Nuclear Energy Liability Insurance Association, Mutual Atomic Energy Liability Underwriters, Nuclear Insurance Association of Canada, or any of their successors.

"Business" Exclusions

Although an exclusion of coverage for activities arising out of a business is common to all the umbrellas surveyed, they are not alike in the treatment of this exclusion, except in one respect. That is, the use of a private passenger auto used for business purposes other than taxi or livery service is covered. So, for example, an insured driving his own auto on sales calls is covered. Likewise, an insured driving a company-furnished car to make sales calls is covered, provided the applicable insurance is in place (see Chapter 4).

A good place to start in examining the umbrella exclusions is the homeowners exclusion. First, the ISO exclusion (1991 edition):

> Coverage E — Personal Liability [does] not apply to bodily injury or property damage:
>
> b. Arising out of or in connection with a business engaged in by an insured. This exclusion applies but is not limited to an act or omission, regardless of its nature or circumstance, involving a service or duty rendered, promised, owed, or implied to be provided because of the nature of the business.
>
> d. Arising out of the rendering of or failure to render professional services.

The ISO homeowners 2000 program contains an exclusion for:

> Bodily injury or property damage arising out of or in connection with a business conducted from an insured location or engaged in by an insured, whether or not the business is owned or operated by an insured or employs an insured.
>
> This Exclusion... applies but is not limited to an act or omission, regardless of its nature or circumstance, involving a service or duty rendered, promised, owed, or implied to be provided because of the nature of the business.

Both the 1991 and 2000 forms exclude coverage for bodily injury or property damage arising out of rendering or failure to render professional services. The AAIS homeowners forms contain the same exclusions for rendering or failure to render professional services, and for activities related to the business (as defined below) of an insured. Problems arise, however, in applying the exclusions, both homeowners and umbrella, because of the different definitions of a business.

The 1991 ISO homeowners form defines a business as including a "trade, profession or occupation." This definition has been changed in the homeowners 2000 program:

> Business means:
>
> a. A trade, profession or occupation engaged in on a full-time, part-time or occasional basis; or
>
> b. Any other activity engaged in for money or other compensation, except the following:
>
> (1) One or more activities, not described in (2) through (4) below, for which no insured receives more than $2,000 in total compensation for the 12 months before the inception date of the policy;
>
> (2) Volunteer activities for which no money is received other than payment for expenses incurred to perform the activity;
>
> (3) Providing home day care services for which no compensation is received, other than the mutual exchange of such services; or
>
> (4) The rendering of home day care services to a relative of an insured.

Although this latter definition is certainly broader than that found in the 1991 homeowners, it leaves unanswered questions that might need clarification in an umbrella. For example, the AAIS definition of a business is:

> Business means a trade, a profession, or an occupation including farming, all whether full or part time.
>
> Business includes services regularly provided by an insured for the care of others and for which an insured is compensated. A mutual exchange of like services is not considered compensation.
>
> Business does not include:
>
> a. part-time or seasonal activities that are performed by minors; or
>
> b. activities that are related to business, but are usually not viewed as business in nature.

And it is this latter clarification, lacking in the ISO definition, that can lead to confusion. An insured, a corporate officer, was on a business trip. While on a break from a seminar, he returned to his hotel room to pack, and inadvertently hit a sprinkler head, setting it off. He caused extensive damage to the room and other areas. The supreme court viewed the "entire transaction as a whole" since he was pursuing his occupation at the time, and therefore the business exclusion applied. The case is *United Food Service, Inc., et al. v. Fidelity and Casualty Company, et al.*, 189 A.D.2d 74 (New York 1993). Had the business definition included terminology like b. above, the outcome might have been different. (Although the exclusion of coverage for "property in the care of an insured" might still have precluded coverage. See below for a discussion of this exclusion and the umbrella response.)

And in the case of *Martinelli v. Security Insurance Company*, 490 S.W.2d 427 (Missouri 1973), Martinelli was injured by a co-worker, Engel, who bumped into him while both were walking on the business premises. The court said that while walking and bumping were normally nonbusiness activities, in the case at hand both occurred in the furtherance of the employer's work. Therefore, the exception for activities viewed as nonbusiness in nature did not apply.

In regards to the activities of minors (a. above in the AAIS homeowners), the ISO homeowners 2000 exclusion for business excepts "an insured under the age of 21 years involved in a part-time or occasional, self-employed business with no employees." Also, neither ISO nor AAIS homeowners forms consider the rental of an insured location for residential or office, garage, school or studio usage to fall within the exclusion. Umbrella forms generally follow suit in that these are not excluded; however, remember that if an insured has residential rental property there must be underlying liability coverage, either by endorsement to the homeowners or with a separate dwelling fire policy.

As noted earlier, umbrella forms are not alike in their treatment of the business exclusion. One reads:

> This policy does not apply to...
>
> 3. any liability arising out of:
>
> (a) any business pursuits or business property of any insured, except for:
>
> (1) the business use of a private passenger automobile or owned watercraft, unless used to carry persons or property for a charge;
>
> (2) the occasional or part-time self-employed business pursuits of any insured who is under 23 years of age [note the two-year age difference between this and the ISO exception, above].
>
> (b) the rendering of any professional service or the omission of such service by any insured.

But another form provides coverage if there is coverage in an underlying policy:

> 1. We will not cover personal injury or property damage arising out of business or business property unless covered under one or more of the basic policies [as noted in the declarations]. We will, however, cover you or a relative for business use of a private passenger car as long as it is not used as a taxi or for hire. We do cover expense sharing or car pooling arrangements.
>
> 2. If anyone covered is a physician, dentist, lawyer, accountant, engineer, architect or other professional person, we will not cover any malpractice, error or omission which is committed in the performance of their profession as such, even if covered by any basic policy.

Agent Tip

Whether or not any insurer wishes to provide umbrella coverage for any business is strictly up to that individual insurer. If there is any question whatsoever, check with the underwriter. Do not assume that all business activities may be covered.

Often distinctions between business and non-business activities blur. Three female co-employees of the insured, a doctor, brought suit for sexual harassment, battery, invasion of privacy and false imprisonment against both the doctor and his employer. State Farm, who insured the doctor under a homeowners and a personal umbrella policy, sought declaratory judgment to determine that it did not have a duty to defend or to indemnify. The trial jury agreed, but the appellate court reversed the decision. The court in *Michael Scheer, M.D., v. State Farm Fire and Casualty Company, et al.*, 708 So. 2d 312 (Florida 1998) said that the complaints that the conduct occurred within the course of his employment were not pertinent to the claims against the doctor individually, but were relevant to the claim against the employer.

The trial court had looked to the case of *Liberty Mutual v. Miller*, 549 So. 2d 1200 (Florida 1989), in which two doctors argued over how to treat a mutual patient. In the course of the argument one pulled the other's stethoscope, apparently inflicting injury. But the appellate court distinguished the case from Scheer, saying that the insured's actions were not related to the insured's profession. (Note that the court did not consider whether the exclusion for intentionally inflicted bodily injury [battery] might have precluded coverage. However, invasion of privacy and false imprisonment are included within the definition of personal injury, so these allegations should have triggered coverage. See Chapter 2 for additional information.)

Activities undertaken as a volunteer, unpaid civic duties, or serving as a director of a not-for-profit organization are not considered business activities. If the insured receives compensation for any of these, however, it can be for no more than expenses. As one form states:

> This personal umbrella liability coverage does not apply to... bodily injury, property damage, or personal injury resulting from an insured's service as an officer or member of a board of directors. However, this exclusion does not apply to bodily injury, property damage, or personal injury resulting from an insured's service as an officer or member of a board of directors for a not-for-profit organization for which the insured is not compensated.
>
> With respect to this exclusion, reimbursement for expenses is not considered compensation.

Agent Tip

Day care, no matter how few the children or how meager the compensation, is still a business for coverage purposes. If your clients provide this service, arrange for coverage.

The Intra-Family Exclusion

Homeowners forms commonly exclude coverage for bodily injury to one insured family member caused by another insured family member. This exclusion of coverage is often called the intra-family exclusion. There are two reasons for this exclusion. One is that such claims disturb domestic harmony; the other is that it places an unfair burden on the insurer to determine if there has been collusion. Therefore, the ISO homeowners forms state:

> Coverage E — Personal Liability, does not apply to... bodily injury to you or an insured within the meaning of part a. [resident relatives] or b. [other persons under the age of 21 in the care of the insured or a resident relative] of 'insured' as defined.

Similarly, the AAIS homeowners forms state:

> Coverage L [personal liability] does not apply to... bodily injury to you, and if residents of your household, your relatives and persons under the age of 21 in your care or in the care of your resident relatives.

The ISO homeowners 2000 program has changed the wording on the exclusion. In addition to the above, the exclusion adds:

> This exclusion also applies to any claim made or suit brought against you or an insured:
>
> 1. To repay; or
>
> 2. Share damages with;
>
> another person who may be obligated to pay damages because of bodily injury to an insured.

The case of *American Family Mutual Insurance Company v. Tamala Jo Ryan et al.*, 330 N.W.2d 113 (Minnesota 1983) demonstrates an application of this exclusion. Tamala Jo, age three, was playing in a neighbor's yard. Her mother was also in the yard working in a garden shared by the two families. The neighbor was mowing his grass using a riding lawn mower, and somehow Tamala Jo fell so that the blades severely damaged her foot and ankle, with the result that she had to have her leg amputated. The Ryans sued the lawn mower manufacturer, who sued them in return alleging negligent supervision and seeking contribution or indemnity. The insureds tendered their defense to their insurer, American Family.

Relying on the exclusion for bodily injury to an insured or to a resident relative of the insured, American Family denied coverage. The case went to the state supreme court, which affirmed that the Minnesota statutes did not prohibit such exclusions, and therefore the household exclusion was valid.

The intra-family exclusion appears in the personal auto policy (PAP) by endorsement in the states where it is allowed. But when endorsement PP 03 23 miscellaneous type vehicle is attached to the auto policy to cover such vehicles as, say, motorcycles and golf carts, the exclusion reappears unless, of course, the state holds such exclusion does not apply.

Umbrella forms generally are as one in excluding bodily injury or personal injury to an insured. One form reviewed was ambiguous, in that the definition of "injury" was:

> Injury means bodily injury or mental harm to others caused by an accident. It also means libel, slander, false arrest, wrongful detention, wrongful eviction or entry, malicious prosecution, humiliation, invasion of privacy, or defamation of character.

Presumably this means that injury caused by an insured *to others* — to those other than insureds — are covered; however, it can easily be argued that the wording can refer to *others who just happen to be insureds*, just as readily.

But, for the most, intra-family exclusions appear in umbrella forms. Such an exclusion may read:

> We do not cover... personal injury [defined as bodily injury or personal injury] to any insured under this endorsement [the umbrella].

Another form contains the exclusion of coverage for:

> ... personal injury [bodily injury and personal injury] to an insured.

Finally, there is:

> Intra-Family Liability. We won't pay vehicle or personal liability for any person for bodily injury to anyone related to that person by blood, marriage or

adoption who is a resident of the same household. This includes a ward or foster child.

But what constitutes "residence" may be a matter left for a court's determination. Mehran Afrasiabi resided in his uncle's house. One day, his uncle and some friends threw him into a swimming pool, which resulted in injury to Mehran. He sued his uncle, but the insurer denied to defend or indemnify based on the intra-family exclusion. The appellate court affirmed the findings of the trial court, that Mehran was a resident of the household. Mehran stated that since he paid rent and had a separate bedroom he maintained a separate household. Not so, said the court. Mehran had full access to the home except for his uncle's bedroom and office, and did not have a separate entrance. The fact he paid rent made no difference, as many grown children living at home paid some compensation their parents. The exclusion, in the case of *Mehran Afrasiabi v. State Farm Fire & Casualty Company*, 73 Cal. App. 4th 1183 (California 1999), was held to be applicable. (See also, "What is a Residence?" p. 26)

Intentional Acts

Homeowners forms exclude bodily injury or property damage intentionally caused. The ISO 1991 homeowners forms exclude coverage for bodily injury or property damage that is "expected or intended by one or more insureds." The AAIS homeowners form excludes:

> bodily injury or property damage:
>
> 1. which is expected by, directed by, or intended by an insured;
>
> 2. that is the result of a criminal act of an insured; or
>
> 3. that is the result of an intentional and malicious act by or at the direction of an insured.
>
> This exclusion applies even if:
>
> 1. the bodily injury or property damage that occurs is different than what was expected by, directed by, or intended by the insured; or
>
> 2. the bodily injury or property damage is suffered by someone other than the person or persons expected by, directed by, or intended by the insured.
>
> However, this exclusion does not apply to bodily injury or property damage that arises out of the use of reasonable force to protect people or property.

There are two obvious differences in these exclusions. First, under the ISO homeowners, there is room to argue that the exclusion applies to the intended injury or damage, and not to an unexpected outcome. The case of *Physicians Insurance Company v. Swanson*, 569 N.E.2d 906 (Ohio 1991) is illustrative. The insured, a teen-ager, was swimming with friends when another group began to insult them. The insured went home, got his father's BB gun, and fired in the direction of the other group. He claimed he was firing at a nearby sign in an attempt to frighten them. But when one teen raised his head to look, a BB struck him in the eye, which resulted in loss of vision. The court held that the insurer could not deny coverage, since the intent to injure was never proved. The AAIS form attempts to close this gap, although it could still be argued that, in the case just reviewed, no bodily injury was ever intended and so the bodily injury that resulted from the intentional act would still be covered.

The other difference in the forms is that, in the AAIS form actions taken to protect persons or property fall outside the exclusion. The importance of this exception is demonstrated by the case of *Auto Owners Insurance Company. v. James Harrington et al.*, 565 N.W.2d 839 (Michigan 1997). One day Brian Tew became extremely drunk, and was overheard threatening to kill someone. He was seen to fire a gun. James Harrington, who lived nearby, was informed of Tew's behavior. Later that night Tew scaled the Harringtons' garage and began to approach the second story window where Harrington's wife and children were. Harrington shot Tew, who later died. The Michigan supreme court held that the intentional act exclusion applied even to acts undertaken in self defense.

The ISO homeowners 2000 forms have addressed this problem:

> Coverages E [personal liability] and F [medical payments to others] do not apply to the following:
>
> 1. Expected or Intended Injury — bodily injury or property damage which is expected or intended by an insured even if the resulting bodily injury or property damage:
>
>   (a) Is of a different kind, quality or degree than initially expected or intended; or
>
>   (b) Is sustained by a different person, entity, real or personal property, than initially expected or intended.

> However, this Exclusion... does not apply to bodily injury resulting from the use of reasonable force by an insured to protect persons or property.

The new exclusion does two things. First, an insured will find it more difficult to argue that, for example, although he hit someone in a bar brawl, he only intended to scare him, not to break his jaw. But second, and most important, reasonable actions taken to protect persons or property are covered.

Finding this same level of coverage in an umbrella form is important, given, unfortunately, today's society. For example, an insured may be pulling out of a parking space when she realizes someone is attempting to force open the driver's side door. In an attempt to scrape off the car-jacker, she intentionally runs into another car. The ISO auto policy (PAP) has no exception that addresses this action. Therefore, an umbrella with the wording below can leave an insured without protection:

> We do not provide coverage for... injury or damage intentionally caused by you, at your direction, or with your knowledge or consent.

An example of umbrella wording that *does* provide coverage for such actions is:

> We do not cover...
>
> 6. Personal injury or property damage due to acts committed by or at an insured's direction with intent to cause personal injury or property damage. This exclusion does not apply to personal injury that results from an act committed to protect persons or property.

Although the above form is broad in its exception, the following is broader still:

> This policy does not apply to...
>
> 15. any act or damage which is expected or intended by any insured, or which is the foreseeable result of an act or omission intended by any insured, which causes personal injury or property damage. But this exclusion does not apply to personal injury resulting from a reasonable action by any insured in:
>
>   (a) preventing or eliminating danger in the operation of motor vehicles or aircraft; or
>
>   (b) protecting persons or property.

One umbrella form gives coverage for:

> ...Bodily injury or property damage resulting from the use of reasonable force by an insured to prevent or eliminate danger in the operation of autos, recreational motor vehicles or watercraft.

Under this last provision, if an insured attempted to take the wheel away from an obviously inebriated dangerous driver, but in so doing ran the car into an embankment, the resulting damage or injury would be covered.

The exclusion for intentional acts can have a great impact on coverage for personal injury; i.e., libel, slander, malicious prosecution, invasion of privacy, or false arrest or detention. These actions are, by their very nature, intentional. It is difficult to think of calling someone a liar, for example, unintentionally. Some umbrellas limit the exclusion to bodily injury or property damage simply by not referencing personal injury. Others state that the exclusion does not apply to personal injury as defined. Still others exclude coverage for libel and slander if the insured knew the libel or slander was false.

Agent Tip

When reviewing coverage for personal injury, make sure that the exclusion for intentional acts does not apply, else the insured could be faced with situations such as those found in *Purelli* and *Bailer* (see Chapter 2).

A final intentional acts exclusion concludes this section:

> Intentional damage or injury. We won't pay liability for any occurrence that an insured person intended to take place, or for any resulting injury whether intended or not.

The exclusion sounds like those above, until the definition of an occurrence is given as:

> Occurrence means the incident that causes an accident or loss. It can be a single event or a series of related events.

Suppose an insured intentionally sits on an antique French commode, accidentally cracking the fragile wood. Under this definition the resulting damage would not be covered. (In July 1999 a commode commissioned by Louis XVI was sold to the French government and returned to the Palace of Versailles. Price at auction — $16.5 million.) Remember, virtually every liability form defines "occurrence" as an accident, and "accident" is given its common dictionary definition of "an unforeseen and unplanned event or circumstance" (*Webster's New Collegiate Dictionary*). The insured intended to sit on the commode; the resulting damage was accidental. What, then, does the above form cover?

Agent Tip

If confronted with this type of language, it is tempting to request clarification from the underwriter. But remember, language controlling coverage provided or excluded is found in the contract, not in an underwriter's clarification. The above language would probably need a court's interpretation, but the insured would bear the cost of proving the point.

Care, Custody, Control

One of the most common "drop down" coverages provided by an umbrella is for property in the care of, rented to, or occupied by, an insured. Remember that homeowners forms give coverage in the property section for personal property owned by or in the care of an insured. There is no liability coverage, except for fire, smoke, or explosion, for damage to property that is rented to, occupied by, used by, or in the care of an insured. (The liability additional coverages provide, regardless of legal liability, up to $500 [AAIS and ISO 1991] or $1,000 [ISO 2000] for damage to property of others. Certain restrictions apply; consult the homeowners forms.) For example, a family rents a vacation condo. The two-year old toddler, joined gleefully by his eight-year old sister, decides to find out what those strange things set in the ceiling are. The water damages not only the rented condo, but also the one below it. Homeowners forms generally do not respond to this loss. (Occasionally a form includes "water" with the fire, smoke, or explosion exception.)

Many umbrella forms fill in this gap in coverage. (But not all. One form will not cover such property "except to the extent that we have agreed to provide insurance by special endorsement.") Keep in mind, though, that other exclusions may be applicable, such as those for damage to watercraft or aircraft, or damage caused intentionally. Some give the coverage by not addressing it at all. Other forms give coverage, but refer to excluded situations. The form below gives coverage for property damage or personal injury arising out of an insured's renting an aircraft with a pilot. However:

> We will not cover property damage to aircraft which is rented to, used by or in the care, custody or control of you or a relative.

The most common way of covering damage to property in an insured's care, custody or control is through excluding coverage only if the insured was contractually obligated to provide insurance, although one form excludes coverage if the insured "promised" to provide insurance. In most forms, however, the coverage grant will take this form:

> The coverages provided by this policy do not apply to...
>
> 16. Property damage to property rented to, occupied or used by, or in the care, custody or control of, the insured to the extent that the insured is obligated by contract to provide insurance for such property. However, this exclusion does not apply to property damage caused by fire, smoke, or explosion.

In the example of the rented condo, above, if the family signed a rental agreement requiring it to provide property coverage, then the sprinkler loss is not covered. However, if the family negligently set fire to the unit, there is coverage in the exception to the exclusion. But in most rental situations, renters or tenants, even those renting a private residence or apartment for any length of time, are not required to provide property insurance, and so the umbrella responds to damage negligently caused by an insured.

But occasionally the exclusion, and exception, are open to interpretation. For example, in the form below it would appear there is coverage:

> This policy will not apply...
>
> 4. to property damage to any:
>
>   (a) property owned by others an insured agreed to insure or be responsible for.

The provision "or be responsible for" is troubling. Renting a hotel room for a night's stay does not involve anything other than a credit card invoice, but signing a rental agreement for an apartment usually means taking responsibility for the rented premises, even if that responsibility means no more than agreeing to leave the premises in the same state they were entrusted to the insured. If all that is intended is to avoid the umbrella's covering property damage to rented or occupied property, then it is less confusing if the umbrella clearly states this:

> We do not cover...
>
> 9. Property damage to:
>
>   (c) Property rented to, used or occupied by, or in the care, custody or control of the insured to the extent that the insured has agreed to provide insurance.

Finally, note that the intent of the "care, custody or control" exclusion and exception is to provide coverage for the property of others. There is no coverage for property damage to property owned by an insured.

Uncommon Exclusions

This coverage guide concludes with a discussion of uncommon exclusions; that is, those found in only a few of the forms surveyed. And, unfortunately, often these exclusions can appear as endorsements attached to the main contract, or buried in other exclusions.

Punitive Damages

One such exclusion is for punitive damages. Of the forms reviewed, only one specifically excluded them:

This policy does not apply to...

20. Any punitive or exemplary damages awarded against any insured.

Violation of a Law

Equally uncommon exclusions are those for violation of a law or for bodily injury or property damage arising out of drugs. One insurer excludes coverage for such occurrences:

This policy does not apply to...

9. Any injury caused by a violation of a penal law or ordinance committed by or with the knowledge or consent of any insured, except those caused by violation of a motor vehicle law.

11. Any personal injury or property damage arising out of the use, sale, manufacture, delivery, transfer or possession by any person of a controlled substance. Controlled substances include but are not limited to cocaine, LSD, marijuana, PCP and all narcotic drugs. However, this exclusion does not apply to the legitimate use of prescription drugs by a person following the orders of a licensed physician.

Note that, in the first exclusion, the insured must have knowledge that he or she is violating the penal law (that is, a law the violation of which involves punishment of some sort) except for a motor vehicle law. The injury must be directly *caused by*, as opposed to *arising out of*, the violation. If injury arising out of such activity were excluded, the result would be that much needed coverage might be denied. For example, think of a person knowingly burning leaves in violation of a local ordinance. The fire gets out of control, and the neighbor's house catches on fire. The damage is actually caused by the fire, but the damage arises out of the insured's willful burning of the leaves. But if the insured is fined for the violation, the policy will not respond to that loss.

The second exclusion precludes coverage for any controlled substance activity. For example, if an insured negligently gives LSD to a friend with the result that the friend thinks he can fly, and dies jumping out a window, there is no coverage.

Pollution and Lead Exclusions

The activity of leaf burning, with its resulting smoke, is a good *segue* into the exclusion for pollution found in some umbrella forms. Many forms are silent, and therefore provide coverage, but an increasing number preclude coverage. Although both the AAIS and the ISO basic homeowners forms do not exclude liability coverage for bodily injury or property damage arising out of pollution or lead contamination, insurers are increasingly apt to attach exclusions. For example, ISO has developed an endorsement that gives limited lead and escaped liquid fuel liability coverage (HO 05 80; form number varies by state). This endorsement illustrates the two areas of major concern to insurers: liability arising out of the ingestion or inhalation of lead, and liability arising out of liquid fuel polluting neighboring premises and ground water.

Although there is a certain degree of similarity to the exclusion found in the commercial general liability form (CGL) for bodily injury or property damage arising out of pollutants, for the most the exclusions in personal umbrella forms are much more all-encompassing. For example, the following exclusion does not contain the exception for fumes or smoke from a hostile fire that is in the CGL form:

This policy does not apply to...

22. Any liability arising, in whole or in part, out of the actual, alleged, or threatened discharge, dispersal, seepage, migration, release, escape, emission, transmission, absorption, ingestion or inhalation of pollutants at any time. This includes any loss, cost or expense arising out of any:

(a) request, demand or order that any insured or others test for, monitor, abate, clean up, remove, contain, treat, detoxify, neutralize, or in any way respond to, or assess, the effects of pollutants;

(b) claim or suit by or on behalf of a governmental authority for damages because of testing for, monitoring, cleaning up, removing, containing, treating, detoxifying, neutralizing, or in any way responding to, or assessing, the effects of pollutants.

"Pollutants" means:

a. liquid fuels;

b. lead or any materials containing lead;

c. asbestos or any materials containing asbestos;

d. radon;

e. formaldehyde or any materials containing formaldehyde;

f. electric fields, magnetic fields, electromagnetic fields, power frequency fields, electromagnetic radiation or any other electric or magnetic energy of any frequency;

g. carbon monoxide; or

h. any other irritant or contaminant, including vapor, fumes, acids, alkalis, chemicals, radioactive substances and waste.

An example of an umbrella form that excludes much the same things, but is less restrictive, is below. Note the exception for heat, smoke or fumes from a hostile fire, absent in the exclusion above:

This personal umbrella liability coverage does not apply to...

12. bodily injury, property damage, or personal injury that results from the actual, alleged, or threatened discharge, dispersal, seepage, migration, release, or escape of pollutants into or upon land, water, or air. However, this exclusion does not apply to:

(a) bodily injury, property damage, or personal injury that results from the heat, smoke, or fumes of a fire on the insured premises that becomes uncontrollable or breaks out from where it was intended to be; or

(b) bodily injury or property damage that arises out of the ownership, leasing, operation, maintenance, use, occupancy, renting, loaning, entrusting, supervision, loading, or unloading of a motor vehicle that is subject to motor vehicle registration or designed for use on public roads, but only to the extent that such bodily injury or property damage is covered by underlying insurance at the time of the occurrence.

13. any loss, cost, or expense arising out of any:

(a) request, demand, or order that any insured or others test for, monitor, clean up, remove, contain, treat, detoxify, neutralize, or in any way respond to or assess the effects of pollutants; or

(b) claim or suit by or on behalf of any governmental authority for damages resulting from testing for, monitoring, cleaning up, removing, containing, treating, detoxifying, neutralizing, or in any way responding to or assessing the effects of pollutants.

16. bodily injury, property damage, or personal injury arising out of lead in any form.

17. any loss, cost, or expense arising out of any:

(a) request, demand, or order that any insured or others test for, monitor, clean up, remove, contain, treat, detoxify, neutralize, or in any way respond to or assess the effects of lead; or

(b) claim of suit by or on behalf of any governmental authority for damages resulting from testing for, monitoring, cleaning up, removing, containing, treating, detoxifying, neutralizing, or in any way responding to or assessing the effects of lead.

In the above form, the definition of a pollutant is:

a. any solid, liquid, gaseous, thermal, or radioactive irritant or contaminant, including acids, alkalis, chemicals, fumes, smoke, soot, vapor, and waste. Waste includes materials to be recycled, reclaimed, or reconditioned, as well as disposed of; and

b. electrical or magnetic emissions, whether visible or invisible, and sound emissions.

Insureds fond of throwing parties with loud, live music beware! Sound emissions are considered "pollutants" and not covered under the above form. But note that there is coverage for injury resulting from a hostile fire, and also for pollution that may result from a motor vehicle subject to motor vehicle registration is there is underlying coverage. For example, an insured watercraft may suffer a ruptured gas line with the result that the surrounding water becomes polluted. If there is responding homeowners or watercraft liability, the umbrella responds as well.

Some forms contain exclusions that are much less sweeping for bodily injury or property damage resulting from pollutants, and therefore provide more coverage. For example:

We do not cover...

13. Personal injury or property damage due to the discharge, dispersal, release, or escape of any irritants, contaminants or pollutants into or upon land, the atmosphere or any watercourse or body of water. This exclusion does not apply:

    (a) If there is underlying liability insurance but our coverage is not broader than the underlying insurance; or

    (b) If the discharge, dispersal, release or escape is sudden and accidental.

Under the above form, there may be underlying coverage, such as ISO endorsement HO 05 80 (see above), and therefore the umbrella may provide coverage on an excess basis. There is also coverage, under the above form, if the pollutants' escape is sudden and accidental. Suppose an insured has a propane tank next to his home, and one day he accidentally knocks the tank over with a riding mower. It rolls down a slight incline, and spews its contents into the next door neighbor's below-grade family room. There is coverage for this accident under the above form, but not so the ones preceding it.

Loss Assessment

Although many umbrella forms are silent as to coverage for loss assessment, there are some that specifically address it by excluding the coverage. As might be expected, neither the American Association of

Insurance Services (AAIS) nor the Insurance Services Office (ISO) personal umbrella forms provide coverage, since both provide coverage in the homeowners. (The basic amounts are ISO, $1,000; AAIS, $1,500. These may be increased.) It is understandable that insurers might wish to limit this exposure, lest they be in the position of providing liability insurance that the master policy should provide.

One form, however, provides coverage, but limits the amount:

> Loss Assessment. We will pay, up to $25,000 in excess of the retained limit, your share of any loss assessment charged during the policy period against you by a corporation or association of property owners. This only applies when the assessment is made as a result of an occurrence covered by this policy.
>
> This coverage applies only to loss assessment charged against you as owner or tenant of the residence premises.
>
> We do not cover loss assessments imposed as a direct or indirect result of any assessment by any government body against you or a corporation or association of property owners.
>
> Regardless of the number of assessments, the limit of $25,000 is the most we will pay for loss arising out of:
>
> a. One accident, including continuous ore repeated exposure to substantially the same general harmful conditions; or
>
> b. A covered act of a director, officer or trustee. An act involving more than one director, officer or trustee is considered to be a single act.

This form limits coverage to $25,000, no matter what umbrella limits are purchased. There is no coverage for a governmental assessment against the corporation or association of property owners. So, for example, if an association of property owners was fined by the local government for contributing to beach erosion or violating pollution laws, the loss assessment coverage will not respond.

Contractual Liability

Both the AAIS and ISO homeowners forms provide contractual liability — that is, liability assumed by an insured — to some extent. The ISO forms state:

Coverage E — Personal Liability, does not apply to:

A. Liability:

(2) Under any contract or agreement. However, this exclusion does not apply to written contracts:

(a) That directly relate to the ownership, maintenance or use of an insured location; or

(b) Where the liability of others is assumed by the insured prior to an occurrence;

unless excluded in (1) above [loss assessment, which is provided elsewhere as an additional coverage] or elsewhere in this policy...

The AAIS forms contain:

Contracts and Agreements — We pay for damages for bodily injury or property damage where the liability of others is assumed by an insured under a written contract:

a. that directly relates to the ownership, maintenance, or use of an insured premises; or

b. if the contract was made before the loss.

The loss causing the bodily injury or property damage must have occurred dur ing the policy period.

If an insured rents a vacation home for a week, or a hall for a wedding reception, and signs a contract agreeing to be responsible for any accidents occurring to others while they are on the premises, there is coverage. Likewise, if an insured contracts with a lawn care service, and the lawn mower man negligently injures a passerby with a rock thrown up by the mower, there is coverage. Note, however, that the forms do not provide coverage if excluded elsewhere. If the lawn care service provider negligently drives a truck onto neighboring premises while on his way to the insured premises and knocks over some trees, there is no coverage since the forms exclude liability for all but insureds that arises out of use of motor vehicles subject to motor vehicle registration.

Contractual liability is not addressed in many forms; therefore it is covered unless another exclusion applies. Difficulties arise, however, when the coverage is addressed, but differently than in an underlying homeowners form. For example, this form excludes liability:

> ...assumed by any insured under any contract or agreement except any indemnity obligation assumed by the insured under a written contract directly relating to the ownership, maintenance or use of the residence premises.

The above form is considerably more restrictive than the homeowners forms, so that it would appear if the insured rented a hall for a wedding reception and signed a hold-harmless agreement, there would be no coverage. Another form limits contractual liability even more strictly:

> This policy will not apply... to any liability of another person assumed by an insured under any contract.

Agent Tip

As noted, the broadest coverage for contractual liability occurs when the issue is not addressed. Some umbrella forms word the coverage provision similarly to those found in the homeowners, thus providing excess liability. Beware of strict exclusions that result in coverage gaps.

And Finally...

Remaining unaddressed are exclusions such as those for sexual molestation or physical abuse. By nature these are considered intentional acts with intent to inflict harm. (For further information, see the *Homeowners Coverage Guide* (National Underwriter, 1999.) Other forms exclude coverage for statutorily imposed liability for bodily injury or property damage resulting from use of a motor vehicle or watercraft, unless covered by underlying insurance. The first group of exclusions is common to homeowners forms as well as personal umbrellas; the second group does not appear with any regularity, and so is not discussed. When considering any umbrella form, review the exclusions carefully so as to avoid any surprises.

Chapter 7

Conditions

Introduction

As might be expected, umbrella forms contain conditions. But here again, as with the coverages and exclusions, there is no real consistency among umbrella forms. This is particularly odd in that conditions are generally much the same from one insurance policy to another in other areas, such as homeowners. Even in commercial forms, where insurers may use the ISO or AAIS forms as springboards to formulate their own policies, it is reasonably expected that there will be no surprises in regard to conditions. Not so with personal umbrellas. Further, conditions do not always conveniently appear in a section called "Conditions." For example, one form divides them into "terms and conditions" and "general conditions." This chapter reviews conditions commonly found in umbrella forms, and notes those that might be expected, but are not found, in all forms. (Cancellation provisions were discussed in Chapter 1.

Maintenance of Underlying Insurance

Although maintenance of underlying insurance was discussed in the first chapter, the importance of this condition cannot be overemphasized. If the insured allows a policy to lapse — say, forgets to pay the homeowners insurance premium — the umbrella policy will not drop down to provide coverage if there is a loss. If the insured is responsible for carrying underlying limits of $300,000 comprehensive personal liability, the umbrella will respond as if these limits were in place. If the usual retained limit is $250, following the lapse it will be $300,250.

Bankruptcy of Underlying Insurer

Unfortunately, if the insured's underlying insurer becomes insolvent, the umbrella insurance will not drop down to fill this coverage gap. Rather, it will respond as if the underlying coverage was in place.

Agent Tip

Make sure than any insureds with personal umbrellas are placed with top-rated carriers. If you suspect a particular insurer may have financial difficulties, promptly move the business from that carrier.

Notification to Insurer

The insured is responsible for notifying the umbrella insurer of any changes to underlying policies. This includes, for example, notification of any additional motor vehicles (the base premium for most umbrella forms is predicated on one home and one car), or a newly acquired watercraft. If the terms of an underlying policy are amended so that coverage becomes restricted in some manner — for example, a driver is excluded because of a poor driving record — the insurer must be notified. Failure to notify an insurer of changes can jeopardize coverage.

Duties After a Loss

Following a loss, there are duties the named insured is required to fulfill. If there is an occurrence that may trigger coverage, or if an insured is sued following an occurrence that may be covered, then the named insured must notify the insurer. Notification to the agent meets this requirement. And, as is common with all liability losses, the insured must forward to the insurer any documents received in connection with the claim, assist the insurer in preparation of a defense, and protect any right of recovery from others.

Defense

Frequently appearing as part of the insuring agreement, but sometimes as a condition or an extra benefit is the insurer's duty to defend after exhaustion of underlying coverage. Obviously, if no underlying policy applies to an occurrence covered by the umbrella, the umbrella insurer will assume the primary defense for a covered claim. The umbrella insurer has the right to join in defense with the underlying insurer if it appears that a suit is likely to involve the umbrella coverage. Some umbrella insurers claim the right to appeal if the insured and underlying insurer elect not to appeal a judgment in excess of the underlying limits. If they make such an appeal, they will do so at their own expense.

Bankruptcy of the Insured

One provision that regularly appears, with much the same wording, is that promising that an insured's insolvency or bankruptcy will not relieve the insurer of any obligation under the policy.

Conformity with State Law

As is common with insurance forms, any terms in them that conflict with state or local laws are amended to conform with the state or local law.

Suit or Action Against the Insurer

For the most, this provision is commonly found in many policies, and it is that the insured may not bring suit against the insurer until all policy provisions have been complied with. Sometimes the provision also states that umbrella insurers cannot be brought into a suit against their own insureds.

Concealment or Fraud

Given the amount of coverage at stake — never less than a million dollars — it would seem that a provision stating that the policy could be voided if the insurer learned of any intentional concealment or misrepresentation of any material fact or circumstances, or any fraudulent conduct relating to the insurance, would be included in every umbrella form. This is not the case, however.

Severability of Insurance

Finally, one would also expect the severability of insurance clause to appear in every umbrella form. It does not. This, remember, is the provision that the insurance applies separately to each insured. However, the limit of liability for any one occurrence is not increased no matter how many claims arise out of one covered occurrence.

Appendix A

Legal Citations

Cases Cited in Chapter 1

United Services Auto Association v. Wilkinson, 569 A.2d 749 (New Hampshire 1989) Uninsured/underinsured motorist must be offered on umbrella, p. 3.

Nationwide Mutual Insurance Co. v. Chivington et al., 595 N.E.2d 1002 (Ohio 1991) Uninsured/underinsured motorist contributes to estate, p. 3.

Lowell K. Wood v. Safeco Insurance Company of America, 980 S.W.2d 43 (Missouri 1998) Negligent misrepresentation, p. 6.

Centennial Insurance Company v. Robert Krutek and Richard Naylor, 1992 U.S. Dist. Lexis 19220 (Illinois 1992) Underlying insurance requirement, p. 7.

Commercial Union Insurance Co. v. Kevin M. Connors et al., 1995 Mass. Super. Lexis 603 (Massachusetts 1995) Importance of policy dates, p. 8.

Cases Cited in Chapter 2

Trinity Universal Insurance Company et al v. Nicole Cowan et al., 945 S.W.2d 819 (Texas 1997) Does mental anguish constitute bodily injury? p. 10.

Wolf et al v. State Farm Insurance Co., 540 A.2d 871 (New Jersey 1988) Emotional distress as bodily injury, p. 11.

Hain et al. v. Allstate Insurance Co., 471 S.E.2d 521 (Georgia 1996) Intentional infliction of emotional distress, p. 15

Frank V. Purrelli v. State Farm Fire and Casualty Company, 698 So. 2d 618 (Florida 1997) Invasion of privacy, p. 15

Byron C. Bailer et al. v. Erie Insurance Exchange, 687 A.2d 1375 (Maryland 1995) Invasion of privacy, p. 16.

Lowell K. Wood v. Safeco Insurance Company of America, 980 S.W.2d 43 (Missouri 1998) Negligent misrepresentation, p. 17.

Safeco Insurance Co. of America v. Andrews, 915 F.2d 500 (California 1990) Negligent misrepresentation, p. 18.

Cases Cited in Chapter 3

United Fire & Casualty v. Reeder et al., 9 F.3d 15 (Louisiana 1993) Ex-spouse as insured, pp. 24-25.

The Midwestern Indemnity Company v. Gerald Craig, et al., 665 N.E.2d 712 (Ohio 1995) Student away at school, p. 27.

Quincy Mutual Fire Insurance Company v. Stephen Clyman, et al., 910 F. Supp. 230 (Pennsylvania 1996) Student away at school, p. 28.

Amica Mutual Insurance Company v. Donegal Mutual Insurance Company, 545 A.2d 343 (Pennsylvania 1988) Where is child's residence when parents divorced? p. 28.

Peggy Mobley v. State Farm Mutual Automobile Ins. Co., 674 So.2d 1117 (Louisiana 1996) Where is child's residence when parents divorced? p. 29.

Robert J. Carbon v. Allstate Insurance Company, 701 So. 2d 462 (Louisiana 1997) Where is child's residence when parents divorced? p. 30.

Allstate Insurance Company v. Mary Jane Sprout et. al, 782 F. Supp. 999 (Pennsylvania 1991) Determinants of residence, p. 31.

State Farm Fire & Casualty Co. v. The Estate of Kenneth John Lazio et. al, 822 F. Supp. 660 (California 1993) Determinants of residence, p. 31.

Hardware Mutual Casualty Company v. Home Indemnity Company, 241 Cal. App. 2d 303 (California 1966) Determinants of residence, p. 32.

Guenther H. Lang et. al v. Foremost Insurance Company, 778 P.2d 510 (Oregon 1989) Resident relatives, p. 32.

Arden B. Engerbretsen et. al v. Arden A. Engerbretsen et. al, 675 A.2d 13 (Delaware 1995) Resident relatives, p. 33.

Cases Cited in Chapter 4

United Services Automobile Association v. William Todd Dunn et al., 598 So. 2d 1169 (Louisiana 1992) Permissive user, p. 40.

Federated Mutual Insurance Company v. Corey Davis et al., 919 F.Supp. 1001 (Mississippi 1995) Permissive user, p. 42.

State Farm Mutual Automobile Insurance Co. v. Moore, 289 So. 3d 909 (Mississippi 1974) Permissive user, p. 43

Industrial Indemnity Company v. Peter Vukmarkovic et al., 562 N.E.2d 1073 (Illinois 1990) Does vehicle fall under "business" exclusion?

Cases Cited in Chapter 5

Orville Douglass et Al. v. Hartford Insurance Company, 602 F.2d 934 (1979 Colorado) Recreational vehicle exclusion held inapplicable, p. 60.

Austin Mutual Insurance Company v. Brian D. Klande et al., 563 N.W.2d 282 (Minnesota, 1997) Motorized vehicle exclusion upheld, p. 60.

Employers Mutual Liability Insurance Company of Wisconsin v. Michigan Mutual Auto Insurance Company, 300 N.W.2d 682 (Michigan 1980) Watercraft exclusion held ambiguous, p. 63.

Cases Cited in Chapter 6

United Food Service, Inc., et al. v. Fidelity and Casualty Company, et al., 189 A.D.2d 74 (New York 1993) Damage to property in care of insured, p. 73.

Martinelli v. Security Insurance Company, 490 S.W.2d 427 (Missouri 1973) Injury to co-worker, p. 73.

Michael Scheer, M.D., v. State Farm Fire and Casualty Company, et al., 708 So. 2d 312 (Florida 1998) Sexual harassment and invasion of privacy, p. 75

Liberty Mutual v. Miller, 549 So. 2d 1200 (Florida 1989) Business pursuits exclusion, p. 75.

American Family Mutual Insurance Company v. Tamala Jo Ryan et al., 330 N.W.2d 113 (Minnesota 1983) Intra-family exclusion, p. 76

Mehran Afrasiabi v. State Farm Fire & Casualty Company, 73 Cal. App. 4th 1183 (California 1999) Intra-family exclusion, p. 78

Physicians Insurance Company v. Swanson, 569 N.E.2d 906 (Ohio 1991) Expected action, unintended result, p. 79.

Auto Owners Insurance Company. v. James Harrington et al., 565 N.W.2d 839 (Michigan 1997) Intentional infliction of bodily injury, p. 79.

Appendix B

Personal Liability Checklist

Date:

Named Insured:
Address:
City/State/Zip:
Phone: **Business** ____________________
Home ____________________

X-date:

Premises Liability:

	Yes	No
Are there any domestic or residence employees?	☐	☐
If yes, is workers compensation required?	☐	☐
Any business activities on residence premises?	☐	☐
Describe:____________________		
Special coverage necessary?	☐	☐
Is there an in-home business?	☐	☐
Is there on-premises day care?	☐	☐
Is professional liability coverage required?	☐	☐
Is any portion of any residence premises rented to others?		
if so, usage:__________________________________		
Are there any unusual pets?	☐	☐

Farming:

	Yes	No
Does insured engage in farming operations? (if yes, specify type)	☐	☐
incidental	☐	☐
custom farming	☐	☐
farm employees	☐	☐
livestock	☐	☐

Motorized Recreational Vehicles:

	Yes	No
Does insured own a snowmobile?	☐	☐
Does insured own an amphibious vehicle?	☐	☐
Does insured own an ATV?	☐	☐
Does insured own a go-kart?	☐	☐
Does insured own a dune buggy?	☐	☐
Does insured own a golf cart?	☐	☐
If yes to any, where used?______________________________		

Watercraft:

	Yes	No
Does insured own a boat/yacht?	☐	☐
sail length:________	☐	☐
power length:________	☐	☐
horsepower:_______		
Is it used for water skiing?	☐	☐
Is it rented to others?	☐	☐
Any jet skis, wet bikes, or the like?	☐	☐
Principal operator(s)/ages:______________________		

Aircraft:

	Yes	No
Does the insured own any aircraft?	☐	☐
How titled:______________________		
How used:______________________		
Is it rented to others?	☐	☐

Rental Residendial Property:

	Yes	No
Does the insured have rental (residential) property?	☐	☐
number of families		
Is there any business conducted on premises?	☐	☐
if so, what?		

Miscellaneous:

	Yes	No
Are there any foster children cared for?	☐	☐
Are there any business activities on premises?	☐	☐
if yes, describe:______________________________		
Does insured volunteer for non-profit org.?	☐	☐
Does the insured have paid civic/public duties?	☐	☐
Is insured a corporate director?	☐	☐
Do insured/insured's children do any babysitting on premises?	☐	☐
Is there a swimming pool on premises?		
if so, is it fenced?	☐	☐
Any other ''attractive nuisances''?	☐	☐
if so, describe__________________		

Personal Automobiles:

List all personal vehicles (include vans and pickups); who drives them; where insured; limits of liability coverage on each; any policy restrictions changing coverage from standard.

	Yes	No
Do insured family members use insured's auto?	☐	☐
Does insured own any pickups or vans?	☐	☐
Does insured own any trailers?	☐	☐
Does insured have any leased autos?	☐	☐
Does insured use nonowned autos?	☐	☐
Does insured use vehicle as a public/livery conveyance?	☐	☐
Is insured's vehicle used by domestic employee(s)?	☐	☐
Is insured's vehicle used for any business purposes?	☐	☐
Is there any other applicable insurance?	☐	☐
Are there any miscellaneous type vehicles (e.g. motorcycles, motorhomes)?	☐	☐

Special Considerations

	Yes	No
Does insured need uninsured/underinsured motorist coverage?	☐	☐
Does the insured have any youthful drivers?	☐	☐
Does insured use auto(s) outside U.S.?	☐	☐

General Comments:

Appendix C

ISO and AAIS Forms

PERSONAL UMBRELLA LIABILITY POLICY

AGREEMENT

In return for payment of the premium and subject to all the terms of this policy, we agree with you as follows:

I. Definitions

A. Throughout this policy, "you" and "your" refer to:

1. The "named insured" shown in the Declarations; and

2. The spouse if a resident of the same household.

B. "We", "us" and "our" refer to the Company providing this insurance.

C. For purposes of this policy, a private passenger type auto, pickup or van shall be deemed to be owned by a person if leased:

1. Under a written agreement to that person; and

2. For a continuous period of at least 6 months.

Other words and phrases are defined. They are in quotation marks when used.

D. "Auto" means:

1. A private passenger motor vehicle, motorcycle, moped or motor home; or

2. While towed by a private passenger motor vehicle, a trailer, farm wagon or farm implement.

E. "Bodily injury" means bodily harm, sickness or disease, including required care, loss of services and death that results.

F. "Business" includes trade, profession or occupation.

G. "Family member" means a resident of your household who is:

1. Your relative, including a ward or foster child; or

2. Under the age of 21 and in the care of you or an "insured" who is age 21 or over.

H. "Fuel System" means:

1. One or more containers, tanks or vessels which have a total combined storage capacity of 100 or more U.S. gallons of liquid fuel; and:

a. Are, or were, located on any single location covered by "underlying insurance"; and

b. Are, or were, used to hold liquid fuel that is intended to be used solely for one or more of the following:

(1) To heat or cool a building;

(2) To heat water;

(3) To cook food; or

(4) To power motor vehicles, other motorized land conveyances or watercraft owned by an "insured";

2. Any pumping apparatus, which includes the motor, gauge, nozzle, hose or pipes that are, or were, connected to one or more containers, tanks or vessels described in Paragraph **H.1.;**

3. Filler pipes and flues connected to one or more containers, tanks or vessels described in Paragraph **H.1.;**

4. A boiler, furnace or a water heater, the liquid fuel for which is stored in a container, tank or vessel described in Paragraph **H.1.;**

5. Fittings and pipes connecting the boiler, furnace or water heater to one or more containers, tanks or vessels described in Paragraph **H.1.**; or

6. A structure that is specifically designed and built to hold the liquid fuel that escapes from one or more containers, tanks or vessels described in Paragraph **H.1.**

I. "Insured" means:

1. You.

2. A "family member".

3. Any person using an "auto", "recreational motor vehicle", or watercraft, which is owned by you and covered under this policy. Any person using a temporary substitute for such "auto" or "recreational motor vehicle" is also an "insured".

4. Any other person or organization but only with respect to the legal responsibility for acts or omissions of you or any "family member" while you or any "family member" is using an "auto" or "recreational motor vehicle" covered under this policy. However, the owner or lessor of an "auto" or "recreational motor vehicle" loaned to or hired for use by an "insured" or on an "insured's" behalf, is not an "insured".

5. With respect to animals owned by you or any "family member", any person or organization legally responsible for such animals. However, a person or organization using or having custody of such animals in the course of any "business" or without the consent of the owner is not an "insured".

J. "Occurrence" means an accident, including continuous or repeated exposure to substantially the same general harmful conditions, which results, during the policy period, in:

1. "Bodily injury"; or
2. "Property damage".

K. "Personal injury" means injury arising out of one or more of the following offenses:

1. False arrest, detention or imprisonment;
2. Malicious prosecution;
3. The wrongful eviction from, wrongful entry into, or invasion of the right of private occupancy of a room, dwelling or premises that a person occupies, committed by or on behalf of its owner, landlord or lessor.
4. Oral or written publication of material that slanders or libels a person or organization or disparages a person's or organization's goods, products or services; or
5. Oral or written publication of material that violates a person's right of privacy.

L. "Property damage" means physical injury to, destruction of, or loss of use of tangible property.

M. "Recreational motor vehicle" means:

1. All-terrain vehicle;
2. Dune buggy;
3. Golf cart;
4. Snowmobile; or
5. Any other motorized land vehicle which is designed for recreational use off public roads.

N. "Retained limit" means:

1. The total limits of any "underlying insurance" or any other insurance that applies to an "occurrence" or offense which:
   a. Are available to an "insured"; or
   b. Would have been available except for the bankruptcy or insolvency of an insurer providing "underlying insurance"; or
2. The deductible, if any, as stated in the Declarations, if the "occurrence" or offense:
   a. Is covered by this policy; and
   b. Is not covered by "underlying insurance" or any other insurance.

O. "Underlying insurance" means any policy providing the "insured" with primary liability insurance covering one or more of the types of liability listed in the Declarations and at limits no less than the retained policy limits shown for those types of liability listed in the Declarations.

II. Coverages

A. Insuring Agreement

We will pay damages, in excess of the "retained limit", for:

1. "Bodily injury" or "property damage" for which an "insured" becomes legally liable due to an "occurrence" to which this insurance applies; and
2. "Personal injury" for which an "insured" becomes legally liable due to one or more offenses listed under the definition of "personal injury" to which this insurance applies.

Damages include prejudgment interest awarded against the "insured".

B. Defense Coverage

1. If a claim is made or a suit is brought against an "insured" for damages because of "bodily injury" or "property damage" caused by an "occurrence" or "personal injury" caused by an offense to which this policy applies, we:
   a. Will provide a defense at our expense by counsel of our choice, even if the suit is groundless, false or fraudulent. However, we are not obligated to defend any suit or settle any claim if:
      (1) The "occurrence" is covered by other "underlying insurance" available to an "insured";
      (2) There is no applicable "underlying insurance" in effect at the time of the "occurrence" or offense and the amount of damages claimed or incurred is less than the applicable deductible amount shown in the Declarations.
   b. May join, at our expense, with the "insured" or any insurer providing "underlying insurance" in the investigation, defense or settlement of any claim or suit which we believe may require payment under this policy.

   However, we will not contribute to the costs and expenses incurred by any insurer providing "underlying insurance"; and

c. Will pay any expense incurred for the "insured's" defense, with our written consent, in any country where we are prevented from defending an "insured" because of laws or other reasons.

2. We may investigate and settle any claim or suit that we decide is appropriate. Our duty to settle or defend ends when the amount we pay for damages in judgment or settlements resulting from the "occurrence" or offense equals our limit of liability.

C. Additional Coverages

In addition to our limit of liability, we will pay:

1. Expenses we incur and costs taxed against an "insured" in any suit we defend;
2. Premiums on bonds required in a suit we defend, but not for bond amounts to the extent they exceed our limit of liability. We need not apply for or furnish any bond; and
3. Reasonable expenses incurred by an "insured" at our request, including actual loss of earnings (but not loss of other income) up to $250 per day, for assisting us in the investigation or defense of a claim or suit; and
4. Interest on our share of the judgment which accrues after entry of the judgment and before we pay or tender, or deposit in court, that part of the judgment which does not exceed the limit of liability that applies.

D. Limit Of Liability

1. Our total liability under this policy for all damages resulting from any one "occurrence" or offense will not be more than the limit of liability as shown in the Declarations of this policy. This limit is the most we will pay regardless of the number of "insureds", claims made, persons injured, or vehicles involved in an accident.

III. Exclusions

A. The coverages provided by this policy do not apply to:

1. "Bodily injury" or "property damage" arising out of an act which is expected or intended by an "insured" to cause "bodily injury" or "property damage". This Exclusion **(A.1.)** applies even if the "bodily injury" or "property damage":

   a. Is of a different kind, quality or degree than expected or intended; or

   b. Is sustained by a different person or entity than expected or intended.

   However, this Exclusion **(A.1.)** does not apply to:

   a. "Bodily injury" resulting from the use of reasonable force by an "insured" to protect persons or property; or

   b. "Bodily injury" or "property damage" resulting from the use of reasonable force by an "insured" to prevent or eliminate danger in the operation of "autos", "recreational motor vehicles" or watercraft;

2. "Personal injury":

   a. Arising out of oral or written publication of material, if done by or at the direction of the "insured" with knowledge of its falsity;

   b. Arising out of oral or written publication of material whose first publication took place before the beginning of the policy period;

   c. Arising out of a criminal act committed by or at the direction of one or more "insureds"; or

   d. Sustained by any person as a result of an offense directly or indirectly related to the employment of this person by the insured;

3. "Bodily injury", "personal injury" or "property damage" arising out of the rental or holding for rental of any part of any premises by an "insured". However, this Exclusion **(A.3.)** does not apply to the rental or holding for rental of:

   a. The residence premises shown in the Declarations:

      (1) On an occasional basis if used only as a residence;

      (2) In part, for use only as a residence, unless a single family unit is intended for use by the occupying family to lodge more than two roomers or boarders; or

      (3) In part, as an office, school, studio or private garage;

   b. Any part of a one to four family dwelling other than the residence premises to the extent that personal liability coverage is provided by "underlying insurance";

   c. A condominium, cooperative, or apartment unit other than the residence premises to the extent that personal liability coverage is provided by "underlying insurance",

4. "Bodily injury", "personal injury" or "property damage" arising out of or in connection with a "business" engaged in by an "insured". This Exclusion **(A.4.)** applies but is not limited to an act or omission, regardless of its nature or circumstance, involving a service or duty rendered, promised, owed, or implied to be provided because of the nature of the "business".

However, this Exclusion **(A.4.)** does not apply to:

a. Civic or public activities performed by an "insured" without compensation other than reimbursement of expenses;

b. An insured minor involved in self-employed "business" pursuits, which are occasional or part-time and customarily undertaken on that basis by minors. A minor means a person who has not attained his or her:

(1) 18th birthday; or

(2) 21st birthday if a full-time student;

c. The providing of home day care service, but only when:

(1) An "insured" renders such service to a relative of an "insured"; or

(2) A mutual exchange of home day care services agreement exists which involves no monetary or other compensation;

d. The use of an "auto" you own, or a temporary substitute for such "auto", by you, a "family member" or a partner, agent or employee of you or a "family member" while employed or otherwise engaged in the "business" of:

(1) Selling;

(2) Repairing;

(3) Servicing;

(4) Storing; or

(5) Parking;

vehicles designed for use mainly on public highways;

e. The use of an "auto" for "business" purposes, other than an auto business, by an "insured". However, we do not provide coverage for liability arising out of the ownership or operation of an "auto" while it is being used as a public or livery conveyance. This Exclusion **(A.4.e)** does not apply to a share-the-expense car pool;

5. "Bodily injury", "personal injury" or "property damage" arising out of the rendering of or failure to render professional services;

6. "Bodily injury" or "property damage" arising from:

a. The ownership, maintenance, use, loading or unloading of an aircraft;

b. The entrustment by an "insured" of an aircraft to any person; or

c. Vicarious liability, whether or not statutorily imposed, for the actions of a child or minor using an aircraft.

An aircraft means any contrivance used or designed for flight, except model or hobby aircraft not used or designed to carry people or cargo;

7. "Bodily injury" or "property damage" arising from:

a. The ownership, maintenance, use, loading or unloading of any watercraft;

b. The entrustment by an "insured" of any watercraft to any person; or

c. Vicarious liability, whether or not statutorily imposed, for the actions of a child or minor using any watercraft.

However, this Exclusion **(A.7.)** does not apply to the extent that watercraft coverage is provided by "underlying insurance" at the time of the "occurrence".

8. "Bodily injury" or "property damage" arising from:

a. The ownership, maintenance, use, loading or unloading of any "recreational motor vehicle" owned by you or any "family member";

b. The entrustment by an "insured" of any "recreational motor vehicle", owned by you or any "family member", to any person; or

c. Vicarious liability, whether or not statutorily imposed, for the actions of a child or minor using any "recreational motor vehicle" owned by you or any "family member".

However, this Exclusion **(A.8.)** does not apply to the extent that "recreational motor vehicle" coverage is provided by "underlying insurance" at the time of the "occurrence".

9. "Bodily injury" or "property damage" caused directly or indirectly by war, including the following and any consequence of any of the following:

a. Undeclared war, civil war, insurrection, rebellion or revolution;

b. Warlike act by a military force or military personnel; or

c. Destruction, seizure or use for a military purpose.

Discharge of a nuclear weapon will be deemed a warlike act even if accidental;

10. A person using an "auto", "recreational motor vehicle" or watercraft without a reasonable belief that that person is entitled to do so. This Exclusion **(A.10.)** does not apply to a "family member" using an "auto", "recreational motor vehicle" or watercraft you own;

11. The use of "autos", "recreational motor vehicles" or watercraft while they are being operated in, or practicing for, any prearranged or organized race, speed contest or other similar competition. However, this Exclusion **(A.11.)** does not apply to:

a. Sailboats; or

b. Watercraft involved in predicted log cruises;

12. "Bodily injury" or "personal injury" to you or any "family member";

13. "Bodily injury" or "personal injury" arising out of:

a. The transmission of a communicable disease by an "insured";

b. Sexual molestation, corporal punishment or physical or mental abuse; or

c. The use, sale, manufacture, delivery, transfer or possession by any person of a Controlled Substance(s) as defined by the Federal Food and Drug Law at 21 U.S.C.A. Sections 811 and 812. Controlled Substances include but are not limited to cocaine, LSD, marijuana and all narcotic drugs. However, this exclusion does not apply to the legitimate use of prescription drugs by a person following the orders of a licensed physician;

14. "Bodily injury", "personal injury" or "property damage" arising out of an act or omission of an "insured" as an officer or member of a board of directors of a corporation or organization. However, this Exclusion **(A.14.)** does not apply if the corporation or organization is not-for-profit and the "insured" receives no compensation other than reimbursement of expenses;

15. "Property damage" to property owned by the "insured";

16. "Property damage" to property rented to, occupied or used by, or in the care, custody or control of, the "insured" to the extent that the "insured" is obligated by contract to provide insurance for such property. However, this Exclusion **(A.16.)** does not apply to "property damage" caused by fire, smoke or explosion;

17. "Bodily injury" to any person eligible to receive any benefits:

a. Voluntarily provided; or

b. Required to be provided;

by an "insured" under any:

a. Workers compensation law;

b. Non-occupational disability law; or

c. Occupational disease law;

18. "Bodily injury" or "property damage" for which an "insured" under this policy:

a. Is also an insured under a nuclear energy liability policy issued by the:

(1) Nuclear Energy Liability Insurance Association;

(2) Mutual Atomic Energy Liability Underwriters; or

(3) Nuclear Insurance Association of Canada;

or any of their successors; or

b. Would be an insured under that policy but for the exhaustion of its limit of liability;

19. "Bodily injury", "personal injury" or "property damage" caused by an "occurrence" or offense involving the escape of fuel from a "fuel system";

20. "Bodily injury" or "personal injury" caused by an "occurrence" or offense involving the absorption, ingestion or inhalation of lead;

21. "Personal injury" or "property damage" caused by an "occurrence" or offense of lead contamination.

B. Liability coverage does not apply to any loss assessment charged against you as a member of an association, corporation or community of property owners.

C. We do not provide:

1. Automobile no-fault or any similar coverage under this policy; or

2. Uninsured Motorists Coverage, Underinsured Motorists Coverage, or any similar coverage unless this policy is endorsed to provide such coverage.

IV. Maintenance Of Underlying Insurance

You must maintain the "underlying insurance" at the full limits stated in the Declarations with no change to more restrictive conditions during the term of this policy. If any "underlying insurance" is cancelled or not renewed and not replaced, you must notify us at once.

If you fail to maintain "underlying insurance", we will not be liable under this policy for more than we would have been liable if that "underlying insurance" was in effect.

V. Duties After Loss

A. In case of an "occurrence" or offense likely to involve the insurance under this policy, the "insured" must give written notice to us or our agent as soon as is practical. Such notice shall set forth:

1. The identity of the policy and "insured";
2. Reasonably available information about the time, place and circumstances of the "occurrence" or offense; and
3. The names and addresses of any claimants and witnesses.

B. If a claim is made or a suit is brought against an "insured", the "insured" must:

1. Notify us immediately in writing;
2. Promptly forward to us every notice, demand, summons or other process relating to the "occurrence" or offense;
3. At our request, help us:
   - **a.** To make settlement;
   - **b.** To enforce any right of contribution or indemnity against any person or organization who may be liable to an "insured";
   - **c.** With the conduct of suits and attend hearings and trials; and
   - **d.** To secure and give evidence and obtain the attendance of witnesses.

C. The "insured" will not, except at the "insured's" own cost, voluntarily make payment, assume obligation or incur expense to others.

VI. General Provisions

A. Appeals

If the "insured" or any insurer providing "underlying insurance" elects not to appeal a judgment which exceeds the "retained limit", we may do so at our own expense. We will pay all costs, taxes, expenses and interest related to our appeal. The amounts we pay will be in addition to our limit of liability.

B. Bankruptcy Of An Insured

Bankruptcy or insolvency of an "insured" will neither:

1. Relieve us of our obligations under this policy; nor
2. Operate to cause this policy to become primary in the event the "insured" is unable to satisfy the "retained limit" either because of insufficient "underlying insurance" or insufficient personal assets.

C. Bankruptcy Of An Underlying Insurer

In the event of bankruptcy or insolvency of any "underlying insurer", the insurance afforded by this policy shall not replace such "underlying insurance", but shall apply as if the "underlying insurance" was valid and collectible.

D. Fraud

We do not provide coverage for any "insured" who has made fraudulent statements or engaged in fraudulent conduct in connection with any "occurrence" or offense for which coverage is sought under this policy.

E. Liberalization Clause

If we make a change which broadens coverage under this edition of our policy without additional premium charge, that change will automatically apply to your insurance as of the date we implement the change in your state, provided that this implementation date falls within 60 days prior to or during the policy period stated in the Declarations.

This Liberalization Clause does not apply to changes implemented through introduction of a subsequent edition of our policy.

F. Other Insurance

The coverage afforded by this policy is excess over any other insurance available to an "insured", except insurance written specifically to be excess over this policy.

G. Our Right To Recover Payment

If we make a payment under this policy, we are entitled to exercise the "insured's" rights of recovery against any person liable for the loss. The "insured" must do nothing after loss to prejudice those rights.

H. Policy Period And Territory

The policy period is stated in the Declarations. This policy applies to an "occurrence" or offense which takes place anywhere in the world.

I. Severability Of Insurance

This insurance applies separately to each "insured". However, this provision will not increase our limit of liability for any one "occurrence" or offense.

J. Suit Against Us

1. No legal action can be brought against us:
   a. Unless there has been full compliance with all the terms of this policy; and
   b. Until the obligation of the "insured" has been determined by final judgment or by agreement signed by us.
2. No person or organization has any right under this policy to join us as a party to any legal action against an "insured".

K. Termination

1. Cancellation By You

You may cancel this policy by:

a. Returning it to us; or

b. Giving us advance written notice of the date cancellation is to take effect.

2. Cancellation By Us

We may cancel this policy only for the reasons stated below by letting you know in writing of the date cancellation takes effect. This cancellation notice may be delivered to you, or mailed to you at your mailing address shown in the Declarations.

Proof of mailing will be sufficient proof of notice.

a. When you have not paid the premium, we may cancel at any time by letting you know at least 10 days before the date cancellation takes effect.

b. When this policy has been in effect for less than 60 days and is not a renewal with us, we may cancel for any reason by letting you know at least 10 days before the date cancellation takes effoot.

c. When this policy has been in effect for 60 days or more, or at any time if it is a renewal with us, we may cancel by letting you know at least 30 days before the date cancellation takes effect.

3. Nonrenewal

We may elect not to renew this policy. We may do so by delivering to you, or mailing to you at your mailing address shown in the Declarations, written notice at least 30 days before the expiration date of this policy. Proof of mailing will be sufficient proof of notice.

4. Other Termination Provisions

c. When this policy is cancelled, the premium for the period from the date of cancellation to the expiration date will be refunded pro rata.

d. If the return premium is not refunded with the notice of cancellation or when this policy is returned to us, we will refund it within a reasonable time after the date cancellation takes effect.

L. Transfer Of Your Interest In This Policy

1. Your rights and duties under this policy may not be assigned without our written consent. However, if you die, coverage will be provided for:
   a. The surviving spouse if resident in the same household at the time of death. Coverage applies to the spouse as if a named insured shown in the Declarations;
   b. Any member of your household who is an "insured" at the time of your death, but only while a resident of the residence premises; or
   c. The legal representative of the deceased person as if a named insured shown in the Declarations. This applies only with respect to the representative's legal responsibility to maintain or use your "autos" or premises covered under this policy.
2. Coverage will only be provided until the end of the policy period.

M. Waiver Or Change Of Policy Provisions

This policy contains all the agreements between you and us. Its terms may not be changed or waived except by endorsement issued by us. If a change requires a premium adjustment, we will adjust the premium as of the effective date of the change.

AAIS
UM 0001 01 00
Page 1 of 11

THIS IS A LEGAL CONTRACT
-- PLEASE READ IT CAREFULLY --

PERSONAL UMBRELLA LIABILITY COVERAGE

The following Table of Contents shows how this policy is organized. It will help "you" locate particular sections of this form.

TABLE OF CONTENTS

Endorsements and schedules may also be part of this policy. They are identified on the "declarations".

Refer to the Definitions for words and phrases that have special meaning. These words and phrases are shown in quotation marks.

AGREEMENT

This policy, subject to all of its "terms", provides the coverages described herein during the policy period. In return "you" must pay the required premium.

AAIS
UM 0001 01 00
Page 2 of 11

DEFINITIONS

1. The words "you" and "your" mean the person or persons named as the insured on the "declarations". This includes "your" spouse if a resident of "your" household.

2. The words "we", "us", and "our" mean the company providing this policy.

3. "Bodily injury" means bodily harm to a person and includes sickness, disease, or death. This also includes required care and loss of services.

   "Bodily injury" does not mean bodily harm, sickness, disease, or death that arises out of:

   a. a communicable disease;

   b. the actual, alleged, or threatened sexual molestation of a person;

   c. mental or emotional injury, suffering, or distress that does not result from physical injury;

   d. physical abuse;

   e. corporal punishment; or

   f. the use, sale, manufacture, delivery, transfer, or possession by any person of Controlled Substances as defined by the Federal Food and Drug Law at 21 U.S.C.A. Sections 811 and 812, including any amendments. Controlled Substances include but are not limited to cocaine, LSD, marijuana, and all narcotic or hallucinogenic drugs. However, this does not apply to the legitimate use of prescription drugs by a person following the orders of a licensed physician.

4. "Business" means a trade, a profession, or an occupation, including farming, all whether full or part time. This includes the rental of property to others.

   "Business" includes services regularly provided by an "insured" for the care of others and for which an "insured" is compensated. A mutual exchange of like services is not considered compensation.

   "Business" does not include:

   a. part time or seasonal activities that are performed by minors; or

   b. activities that are related to "business", but are usually not viewed as "business" in nature.

5. "Declarations" are all pages labeled Declarations, Supplemental Declarations, or Schedules that pertain to this policy.

6. "Domestic employee" means a person employed by an "insured" to perform duties that relate to the use and care of the "insured premises". This includes a person who performs duties of a similar nature elsewhere for an "insured". This does not include a person while performing duties in connection with the "business" of an "insured".

7. Except as stated within this definition, "insured" means all persons or entities covered by "underlying insurance". Each such person or entity is a separate "insured", but this does not increase "our" "limit".

   No person is an "insured" with respect to the use of a "motorized vehicle", watercraft, or trailer unless that person has a reasonable expectation that he or she has a right to such use. However, this does not apply to the use of a "motorized vehicle", watercraft, or trailer that "you" own or lease by a person who is:

   a. "your" relative and a resident of "your" household; or

   b. under the age of 21, residing in "your" household, and in "your" care or in the care of "your" resident relatives.

8. "Insured premises" means all premises covered by "underlying insurance".

9. "Limit" means the amount of coverage that applies.

10. "Motorized vehicle" means a self-propelled land or amphibious vehicle regardless of method of surface contact. This does not include vehicles that are designed and used to assist the handicapped and are not required to be licensed for road use.

11. "Occurrence" means an accident, including repeated exposures to similar conditions, that results in "bodily injury" or "property damage" during the policy period.

12. "Personal injury" means false arrest, false imprisonment, wrongful eviction, wrongful entry, wrongful detention, malicious prosecution, misrepresentation, libel, slander, defamation of character, or invasion of privacy.

    "Personal injury" does not mean false arrest, false imprisonment, wrongful eviction, wrongful entry, wrongful detention, malicious prosecution, misrepresentation, libel, slander, defamation of character, or invasion of privacy that arises out of:

    a. a communicable disease; or

    b. the actual, alleged, or threatened sexual molestation of a person.

13. "Pollutant" means:

    a. any solid, liquid, gaseous, thermal, or radioactive irritant or contaminant, including acids, alkalis, chemicals, fumes, smoke, soot, vapor, and waste. Waste includes materials to be recycled, reclaimed, or reconditioned, as well as disposed of; and

    b. electrical or magnetic emissions, whether visible or invisible, and sound emissions.

14. "Property damage" means:

    a. physical injury or destruction of tangible property; or

    b. the loss of use of tangible property whether or not it is physically damaged.

15. "Suit" means any civil proceeding in a court of law in which damages because of "bodily injury", "personal injury", or "property damage" to which this insurance applies are sought.

    "Suit" may also include arbitration proceedings in which damages for "bodily injury", "personal injury", or "property damage" are claimed and to which the "insured" must submit or does submit with "our" consent, or any other alternative dispute resolution proceeding in which such damages are claimed and to which the "insured" does submit with "our" consent.

16. "Terms" means all provisions, limitations, exclusions, conditions, "declarations", and definitions used in this policy.

17. "Underlying insurance" means the liability insurance coverage provided under policies shown in the Schedule of Underlying Insurance on the "declarations" for the "limits" and policy periods indicated. It includes any policies issued to replace those policies during the term of this policy that provide:

    a. at least the same "limits"; and

    b. the same hazards insured against, except as modified by general program revisions or as agreed to by "us" in writing.

18. "Underlying insurer" means any insurer who issues a policy of "underlying insurance".

PRINCIPAL COVERAGE

"We" pay, up to "our" "limit", all sums for which an "insured" is liable by law because of "bodily injury", "personal injury", or "property damage" to which this Personal Umbrella Liability Coverage applies.

No other obligation or liability to pay sums or perform acts or services is covered unless explicitly provided for under Defense Coverage.

Subject to the Exclusions, this insurance applies only to:

1. "bodily injury" and "property damage" that is caused by an "occurrence"; and

2. "personal injury" arising from an offense committed during the policy period.

DEFENSE COVERAGE

1. "We" have the right to defend, investigate, and settle any claim or "suit" seeking damages covered by this policy. "We" may elect at any time to participate with the "insured" and with any "underlying insurer" or other insurer in the defense, investigation, and settlement of any claim or "suit" arising out of an "occurrence" or an offense that, in "our" opinion, may involve damages to which this policy may apply. However, "we" have no obligation to share in or contribute to any costs or expenses incurred by any "underlying insurer" or other insurer.

2. "We" have the duty to defend any claim or "suit" seeking damages to which this insurance applies, but only with respect to damages:

   a. covered by "underlying insurance" or any other valid and collectible insurance available to the "insured" except for exhaustion of a "limit" by the payment of losses; or

   b. not covered by "underlying insurance" or any other valid and collectible insurance available to the "insured". However, "we" have no duty to defend a claim or "suit" seeking damages for an amount that does not exceed the Retained Limit shown on the "declarations".

   "Our" duty to defend ends when "we" have paid an amount equal to "our" "limit" as a result of a judgment or written settlement.

   If "we" are prevented by law or otherwise prevented from carrying out this agreement, "we" will pay the "insured" for any expense incurred with "our" written consent.

3. If "we" defend a "suit", "we" pay:

   a. the costs taxed to an "insured";

   b. the costs incurred by "us";

   c. the actual loss of earnings by an "insured" for time spent away from work at "our" request ("We" pay up to $100 per day.);

   d. the necessary costs incurred by "you" at "our" request;

   e. the interest that accrues after the entry of a judgment, but ending when "we" tender or pay up to "our" "limit";

   f. the premiums on appeal bonds or bonds for the release of attachments up to "our" "limit" ("We" are not required to apply for or furnish bonds.);

   g. the premiums up to $500 per bail bond required of an "insured" because of an accident or a traffic law violation arising out of the use of a vehicle to which this policy applies ("We" are not required to apply for or furnish bonds.); and

h. prejudgment interest awarded against an "insured" on that part of the judgment "we" pay. If "we" offer to pay the "limit", "we" will not pay any prejudgment interest based on that period of time after the offer.

These payments will not reduce the "limit" as described under How Much We Pay.

EXCLUSIONS

This Personal Umbrella Liability Coverage does not apply to:

1. "bodily injury" or "property damage" that results from the ownership, leasing, operation, maintenance, use, occupancy, renting, loaning, entrusting, supervision, loading, or unloading of aircraft. However, this exclusion does not apply to:

   a. "bodily injury" to a person while performing duties as a "domestic employee"; or

   b. model aircraft not designed or used to carry people or cargo.

2. liability imposed by law on an "insured" for "bodily injury" or "property damage" that results from the use of:

   a. a "motorized vehicle", watercraft, or trailer by another person. However, this exclusion does not apply to the extent that such liability is covered by "underlying insurance" at the time of the "occurrence"; or

   b. an aircraft by another person.

3. "bodily injury" or "property damage" that results from the ownership, leasing, operation, maintenance, use, occupancy, renting, loaning, entrusting, supervision, loading, or unloading of "motorized vehicles" or trailers. Except as stated in the following paragraph, this exclusion does not apply to the extent that such "bodily injury" or "property damage" is covered by "underlying insurance" at the time of the "occurrence".

   Regardless of the "terms" of the "underlying insurance", this Personal Umbrella Liability Coverage does not provide:

   a. automobile no fault or any similar coverage;

   b. uninsured motorists coverage or underinsured motorists coverage or any similar coverage; or

   c. automobile medical expense, automobile medical payments, or any similar coverage.

4. "bodily injury" or "property damage" that results from the ownership, leasing, operation, maintenance, use, occupancy, renting, loaning, entrusting, supervision, loading, or unloading of watercraft. Except as stated in the following paragraph, this exclusion does not apply to the extent that such "bodily injury" or "property damage" is covered by "underlying insurance" at the time of the "occurrence".

   Regardless of the "terms" of the "underlying insurance", this Personal Umbrella Liability Coverage does not apply to "bodily injury" or "property damage" that results from the use of watercraft in or in the practice or the preparation for any prearranged or organized racing, speed, or stunt activities or contests. This does not apply to watercraft used in predicted log cruises or to sailing vessels.

5. "bodily injury", "property damage", or "personal injury" that results from activities related to the "business" of any "insured", whether or not the "bodily injury", "property damage", or "personal injury" is covered by "underlying insurance" at the time of the "occurrence" or offense. However, this exclusion does not apply to:

   a. with respect to an "insured premises" normally occupied by "your" household:

      1) the occasional rental or holding for rental for use as a residence of that part of the "insured premises" normally occupied solely by "your" household; or
      2) the rental or holding for rental for use as a residence of part of the "insured premises" not normally occupied solely by "your" household, but only if no family unit houses more than two roomers or boarders;

   b. the rental or holding for rental, in whole or in part, of an "insured premises", other than an "insured premises" described in 5.a.1) or 5.a.2) above, for use as a residence;

   c. the rental or holding for rental of part of an "insured premises" for use as a school, studio, office, or private garage; or

   d. the use of a "motorized vehicle" or a trailer, but only to the extent that such use is covered by "underlying insurance" at the time of the "occurrence" or offense.

6. "bodily injury", "property damage", or "personal injury" assumed by an "insured" under any contract or agreement. However, this exclusion does not apply:

   a. where the liability of others is assumed by an "insured" under a written contract that directly relates to the ownership, maintenance, or use of an "insured premises"; or

   b. to the extent that such "bodily injury", "property damage", or "personal injury" is covered by "underlying insurance" at the time of the "occurrence" or offense.

7. "property damage" to property owned by an "insured".

8. "property damage" to any property for which an "insured" is contractually obligated to provide insurance at the time of the "occurrence". However, this exclusion does not apply to "property damage" caused by fire, smoke, or explosion.

9. "bodily injury" or "property damage":

   a. that is expected by, directed by, or intended by an "insured";

   b. that is the result of a criminal act of an "insured"; or

   c. that is the result of an intentional and malicious act by or at the direction of an "insured".

   This exclusion applies even if the "bodily injury" or "property damage" that occurs is different than what was expected by, directed by, or intended by the "insured"; or is suffered by someone other than the person or persons expected by, directed by, or intended by the "insured". However, this exclusion does not apply to "bodily injury" or "property damage" that arises out of the use of reasonable force to protect people or property.

10. "bodily injury" or "personal injury" to "you" and, if residents of "your" household, to "your" relatives and to persons under the age of 21 in "your" care or in the care of "your" resident relatives.

11. "bodily injury" or "property damage" that results from premises that are owned, rented, or controlled by an "insured" and that are not "insured premises". However, this exclusion does not apply to the extent that such "bodily injury" or "property damage" is covered by "underlying insurance" at the time of the "occurrence".

12. "bodily injury", "property damage", or "personal injury" that results from the actual, alleged, or threatened discharge, dispersal, seepage, migration, release, or escape of "pollutants" into or upon land, water, or air. However, this exclusion does not apply to:

    a. "bodily injury", "property damage", or "personal injury" that results from the heat, smoke, or fumes of a fire on the "insured premises" that becomes uncontrollable or breaks out from where it was intended to be; or

    b. "bodily injury" or "property damage" that arises out of the ownership, leasing, operation, maintenance, use, occupancy, renting, loaning, entrusting, supervision, loading, or unloading of a motor vehicle that is subject to motor vehicle registration or designed for use on public roads, but only to the extent that such "bodily injury" or "property damage" is covered by "underlying insurance" at the time of the "occurrence".

13. any loss, cost, or expense arising out of any:

    a. request, demand, or order that any "insured" or others test for, monitor, clean up, remove, contain, treat, detoxify, neutralize, or in any way respond to or assess the effects of "pollutants"; or

    b. claim or "suit" by or on behalf of any governmental authority for damages resulting from testing for, monitoring, cleaning up, removing, containing, treating, detoxifying, neutralizing, or in any way responding to or assessing the effects of "pollutants".

14. "bodily injury", "property damage", or "personal injury" that results from the rendering of or the failing to render a professional service.

15. "bodily injury" or "property damage" that results from the use of a "motorized vehicle" or a trailer in or in the practice or the preparation for racing, speed, pulling or pushing, demolition, or stunt activities or contests.

16. "bodily injury", "property damage", or "personal injury" arising out of lead in any form.

17. any loss, cost, or expense arising out of any:

    a. request, demand, or order that any "insured" or others test for, monitor, clean up, remove, contain, treat, detoxify, neutralize, or in any way respond to or assess the effects of lead; or

    b. claim or "suit" by or on behalf of any governmental authority for damages resulting from testing for, monitoring, cleaning up, removing, containing, treating, detoxifying, neutralizing, or in any way responding to or assessing the effects of lead.

18. "bodily injury", "property damage", or "personal injury" resulting from an "insured's" service as an officer or member of a board of directors. However, this exclusion does not apply to "bodily injury", "property damage", or "personal injury" resulting from an "insured's" service as an officer or member of a board of directors for a not for profit organization for which the "insured" is not compensated.

    With respect to this exclusion, reimbursement for expenses is not considered compensation.

19. "bodily injury" or "property damage" that results from war. (This includes undeclared war, civil war, insurrection, rebellion, revolution, warlike act by a military force or military personnel, or destruction, seizure, or use of property for a military purpose. Discharge of a nuclear weapon is deemed a warlike act even if accidental.)

20. "bodily injury" or "property damage" that results from an "occurrence" for which an "insured" is also an insured under a nuclear energy liability policy or would be an insured but for the exhaustion of its "limits". (A nuclear energy liability policy is a policy issued by the American Nuclear Insurers, Mutual Atomic Energy Liability Underwriters, Nuclear Insurance Association of Canada, or their successors.)

21. "bodily injury" to a person, including a "domestic employee", if the "insured" has a workers' compensation policy covering the injury or if benefits are payable or are required to be provided by the "insured" under a workers' compensation, non-occupational disability, occupational disease, or like law.

22. liability for any assessment made by "your" homeowners, condominium, mobile-homeowners, or similar residential association.

23. "personal injury" that results from the willful violation of a law or ordinance by, at the direction of, or with the knowledge or consent of an "insured".

24. "personal injury" to a person that results from an offense directly or indirectly related to the person's employment by an "insured".

25. "personal injury" caused by a publication, statement, or act by, at the direction of, or with the knowledge or consent of an "insured" before the effective date of this insurance.

26. "personal injury" caused by a publication or statement made by, at the direction of, or with the knowledge or consent of an "insured", if the "insured" knew or had reason to believe that the publication or statement was false.

WHAT YOU MUST DO IN CASE OF LOSS

1. "You" must cooperate with the "underlying insurers" as required by the terms of their policies and comply with all terms and conditions of those policies.

2. "You" must see to it that "we" receive notice as soon as practical of an "occurrence" or an offense to which this insurance may apply. The notice to "us" must state:

   a. the name of the "insured"; the policy number; and the time, place, and details of the "occurrence" or offense; and

   b. the names and addresses of all known potential claimants and witnesses.

3. **Cooperation** -- The "insured" must cooperate with "us" in performing all acts required by this policy.

4. **Volunteer Payments** -- An "insured" must not make payments, pay or offer rewards, or assume obligations or other costs except at the "insured's" own cost.

5. **Other Duties** -- In case of an "occurrence" or offense that might result in a claim, the "insured" must promptly give "us" copies of all notices, demands, and legal papers that relate to the "occurrence", offense, or claim.

   At "our" request, the "insured" must help "us":

   a. to settle a claim;

   b. to conduct "suits" (This includes being at trials and hearings.);

   c. to enforce the right of recovery or indemnification against all parties who may be liable to an "insured" for the injury or damage;

d. in the securing of and giving of evidence; and

e. in obtaining the attendance of all witnesses.

HOW MUCH WE PAY

The "limit" shown on the "declarations" for this Personal Umbrella Liability Coverage is the most "we" pay for loss for each "occurrence" or offense. This applies regardless of the number of:

1. persons insured under this policy;

2. parties who sustain injury or damage;

3. claims made or "suits" brought; or

4. vehicles, watercraft, or trailers involved in an accident.

EXCESS INSURANCE

1. **Other Insurance** -- The insurance provided by this policy is excess over "underlying insurance", whether or not valid and collectible, and any other valid and collectible insurance available to the "insured", except insurance that is specifically purchased by the "insured" as excess insurance over the insurance provided by this policy.

   If there is no "underlying insurance" or valid and collectible insurance available to the "insured" with respect to an "occurrence" or offense to which the insurance provided by this policy applies, then this insurance will apply as excess over the Retained Limit shown on the "declarations", except when:

   a. the "underlying insurer" is bankrupt or insolvent as stated below under item 3., Bankruptcy of Underlying Insurer; or

   b. "you" fail to maintain "underlying insurance" as stated under Condition 8., Maintenance of Underlying Insurance.

2. **Failure To Maintain Underlying Insurance** -- If "you" fail to maintain "underlying insurance" as required by Condition 8., Maintenance of Underlying Insurance, the insurance provided by this policy will not replace such "underlying insurance" but will apply as if the "underlying insurance" were valid and collectible.

3. **Bankruptcy Of Underlying Insurer** -- In the event of bankruptcy or insolvency of any "underlying insurer", the insurance provided by this policy will not replace such "underlying insurance", but will apply as if the "underlying insurance" were valid and collectible.

CONDITIONS

1. **Appeals** -- If an "underlying insurer" elects not to appeal a judgment in excess of the "limit" of any "underlying insurance", "we" may elect to make such appeal. If "we" so elect, "we" will be liable, in addition to the applicable "limit", for all expenses "we" incur that pertain to such appeal.

2. **Bankruptcy Of An Insured** -- Bankruptcy or insolvency of an "insured" does not relieve "us" of "our" obligations under this policy.

3. **Cancellation and Nonrenewal** -- "You" may cancel this policy by returning the policy to "us" or by giving "us" written notice and stating at what future date coverage is to stop.

   "We" may cancel or not renew this policy by written notice to "you" at the address shown on the "declarations". Proof of delivery or mailing is sufficient proof of notice.

   If "we" cancel this policy during the first 60 days that it is in effect, "we" will give "you" notice at least ten days before cancellation is effective.

If "we" cancel this policy after it has been in effect 60 days or more or if it is a renewal of a policy issued by "us", "we" will give "you" notice:

a. at least ten days before cancellation is effective, if cancellation is because the premium has not been paid when due; or

b. at least 30 days before cancellation is effective, if cancellation is for any reason other than nonpayment of premium.

If "we" do not renew this policy, "we" will give "you" notice at least 30 days before nonrenewal is effective.

"Your" return premium, if any, will be refunded at the time of cancellation or as soon as practical. Payment or tender of the unearned premium is not a condition of cancellation.

4. **Change, Modification, or Waiver of Policy Terms** -- A waiver or change of the "terms" of this policy must be issued by "us" in writing to be valid.

   If "we" adopt a revision that broadens coverage under this edition of "our" policy without an additional premium, the broadened coverage will apply to "your" policy as of the date "we" adopt the revision in the state in which "your" mailing address shown on the "declarations" is located. This applies only to revisions adopted 60 days prior to or during the policy period shown on the "declarations". This does not apply to changes adopted as a result of the introduction of a subsequent edition of "our" policy.

   "Our" request for an appraisal or examination under oath does not waive policy "terms".

   If this policy has no expiration date, "we" may substitute or "we" may add, at each anniversary date, forms that are then authorized for use.

5. **Conformity With Statute** -- "Terms" in conflict with the laws of the state in which "your" mailing address shown on the "declarations" is located are changed to conform to such laws.

6. **Inspections** -- "We" have the right, but are not obligated, to inspect "your" property and operations. This inspection may be made by "us" or may be made on "our" behalf. An inspection or its resulting advice or report does not warrant that "your" property or operations are safe, healthful, or in compliance with laws, rules, or regulations. Inspections or reports are for "our" benefit only.

7. **Legal Action Against Us** -- No legal action may be brought against "us" unless:

   a. all the "terms" of this policy have been complied with; and

   b. the amount of an "insured's" liability has been fixed by:

      1) a final judgment against an "insured" as a result of a trial; or
      2) a written agreement of the "insured", the claimant, and "us".

   No person has a right under this policy to join "us" or implead "us" in actions that are brought to fix the liability of an "insured".

8. **Maintenance Of Underlying Insurance** -- "You" must maintain the "underlying insurance" in full force and effect during the term of this policy.

   If any "underlying insurance" is canceled or not renewed and not replaced or is at any time materially changed in "limits" or coverages, "you" must notify "us" at once. "We" will not be liable under this policy for more than "we" would have been liable if that "underlying insurance" had not been terminated or had been kept at its original "limits" or coverages.

Reduction or exhaustion of any aggregate "limit" in any "underlying insurance" by payments for judgments, settlements, or expenses for "occurrences" or offenses during the policy period of this policy will not be a failure to maintain "underlying insurance" in full force and effect.

No statement contained in this condition limits "our" right to cancel or not renew this policy.

9. **Misrepresentation, Concealment, or Fraud** -- This coverage is void as to "you" and any other "insured" if before or after a loss:

   a. "you" or any other "insured" has willfully concealed or misrepresented:

      1) a material fact or circumstance that relates to this insurance or the subject thereof; or
      2) the "insured's" interest herein; or

   b. there has been fraud or false swearing by "you" or any other "insured" with regard to a matter that relates to this insurance or the subject thereof.

10. **Subrogation** -- If "we" pay for a loss, "we" may require that "you" assign to "us" the right of recovery up to the amount "we" pay. "We" are not liable for a loss if, after the loss, "you" impair "our" right to recover against others. "You" may waive "your" right to recover, in writing, before a loss occurs, without affecting coverage.

11. **Transfer Of Your Rights And Duties Under This Policy** -- "Your" rights and duties under this policy may not be transferred without "our" written consent except in the case of "your" death.

    If "you" die, "your" rights and duties will be transferred to "your" legal representative but only while acting within the scope of duties as "your" legal representative. Until "your" legal representative is appointed, anyone having proper temporary custody of "your" property will have "your" rights and duties but only with respect to that property.

Index

D

E

F

G

H

I

L

M

N

O

P

R

S

U

V

W